In the Shadow of the Mountain

FISHING Mount Hood Country

Authors:
By Gary Lewis
Robert H. Campbell

Editors:
Merrilee Lewis
Larry McGlocklin

Contributors:
Terry Otto, Blake Miller,
Dave Kilhefner, Tye Krueger

Photography:
Gary Lewis, Robert Campbell,
Mark Bachmann, Jake Carse

Cover Design:
Pete Chadwell, Dynamic Arts

Book Design & Production:
Pete Chadwell, Dynamic Arts

Ad Design:
Jennifer Lewis
Pete Chadwell, Dynamic Arts

Accounts:
Dave Jones, Brian Davis

About the Cover:
Sandy River steelhead.
Photo by Dave Kilhefner

Gary Lewis Outdoors
P.O. Box 1364
Bend, Oregon 97709
www.garylewisoutdoors.com

We live in the shadow of The Mountain. On clear days it calls us, visible from any high spot in Portland. It looms above the Columbia, shrouded in fog, it beckons from the plains of the Warm Springs.

Seven-hundred-thousand-years-old, the geologists say, Oregon's tallest peak is a stratovolcano, a volcanic mountain of lava and ash heaved against the sky. At 11,239 feet above sea level, it ranks fourth among the prominent points in the whole of the Cascade Range.

In 1792, Lieutenant William Broughton, sailing with George Vancouver to the mouth of the Columbia, named the distant peak for British Admiral Samuel Hood. In 1805, traveling down the Columbia from the east, Lewis and Clark spotted the mountain and called it Falls Mountain and Timm Mountain. Timm was the native name for Celilo Falls.

From their camps north and west of the mountain, the Multnomah tribe named the mountain Wy'east, a son of the Great Spirit. From Parkdale to Portland, from Maupin to Molalla, from Corbett to Clackamas, it is simply called The Mountain.

From any angle, even in August, snow and ice can be seen in the crevasses. Twelve glaciers, which cover over 3,000 acres, can be counted on Hood's flanks. Six major rivers originate in the ice fields and the founts that spring up from the ground. Coalman glacier, located between Crater Rock and the summit is one of the smallest, at 20 acres. Palmer, at 32 acres is the source of the trickle that is at the headwater of the Salmon River.

On the east side of the mountain, the 133-acre White River glacier is the supply of the White River, which in turn drains into the Deschutes. To the north lies the Newton Clark glacier where the East Fork Hood River begins. Eliot glacier feeds Tilly Jane Creek and the Eliot Branch, both tributary to the Middle Fork Hood River. Langille, Coe and Ladd

Six major rivers originate in the snowmelt on Mount Hood, but many of the best fisheries are only accessible on foot with a rod and a map and compass in hand.
Photo by Rodney Smith.

glaciers also feed into the Hood River watershed.

On the west side, the Glisan, Sandy and Reed glaciers feed the Sandy River, while the Zigzag becomes the Zigzag River.

According to the geologic history, Wy'east's most recent volcanic event occurred in the 1790s. A flow of mud and boulders and pyroclastic material bowled through fir trees and cedars, down the Sandy River, all the way to the Columbia. In 1805, when Lewis and Clark charted the mouth of the river, they called it the Quicksand.

The Oak Grove Fork of the Clackamas originates in Timothy Lake. From the south flank, the Salmon River gathers water out of dozens of little creeks as it makes its long turn west and north to the Sandy. Crashing down the mountain, the Zigzag River runs parallel to the Mount Hood Highway to join the Sandy north of the town of Zigzag.

Carrying glacial silt, the Sandy scribes the north side of Zigzag Mountain then winds west and then north. The Bull Run is a 22-mile tributary that heads in Bull Run Lake near Hiyo Mountain.

On the north and east sides of the mountain, the forks of the Hood River gather water from the glaciers and tributaries to flow north to the Columbia at Hood River.

Sloping east from the Pacific Crest, the White River drains south then east to the Deschutes.

These rivers support runs of chinook and coho salmon, steelhead and sea-run cutthroat. In the upper rivers and in creeks, lakes and ponds, resident rainbows, bull trout, brook trout, brown trout and West Slope cutthroat trout can be found. On the shoulders of the mountain, and in its shadow, there are more rivers to walk and miles of lakeshore than one angler could prospect in one lifetime. Lakes and creeks wink blue like so many sapphires strewn on velvet and speckled trout dance like jewels caught in the current.

In this book we hope to introduce the angler to the myriad waters and communities on the slopes of the mountain. We do not cover all of the lakes and streams of the Mount Hood National Forest, rather we highlight some and let you seek out your own gems. Along the way, we hope you will visit our sponsors, the advertisers that helped make this book possible. Be sure you tell them you heard about them in Fishing the Mount Hood National Forest.

Mount Hood Country

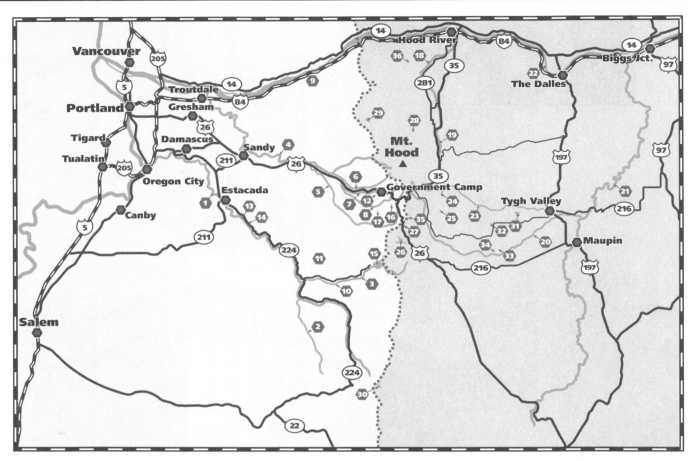

Table of Contents

For Lily and Robin:
May our wild places keep you
forever young, forever free.

Dad

Clackamas River

Origin ....Cascade Mountains; Olallie Butte

Length................................. ~83 miles

Regulations .... All salmon and steelhead must have a healed adipose fin clip in order to retain.

Terminus .... Flows into the Willamette River at Oregon City

Elevation at source .... ~4,900 feet

Elevation at mouth .... ~10 feet

Species: Summer and winter steelhead, spring chinook, coho, cutthroat and rainbow trout, re-introduced bull trout. Shad are occasional visitors in June/July.

Best Methods: Side-drifting for steelhead; back-bouncing for chinook; bobber-fishing eggs for coho; fly fishing for trout

Tips: The Clackamas fishes best for salmon and steelhead from 11 to 13 feet on the Estacada river gauge.

The Clackamas River is yet another stream conveniently located near the Portland metropolitan area providing countless recreational opportunities for the people of Oregon's most populated region. For practical reasons, the Clackamas is often characterized by its "upper" and "lower" sections. The upper river above the dams is a clear-flowing, rowdy mountain stream laced with gnarly rapids and having a wild disposition. The lower river, below the dams and the town of Estacada, is a large, powerful river that harbors a variety of fish runs that provide year-round fishing for the metro-area angler.

The Clackamas begins life in the Olallie Lake area between Mt Hood and Mt Jefferson. Olallie is a Chinook jargon word for berry, which are common in the area during summer and fall. The river starts as a diminutive mountain creek but grows quickly as it absorbs the flow of its many tributaries. Cascades Scenic Byway No. 46 picks up the Clackamas near its headwaters just west of Warm Springs Indian Reservation and follows the stream to the junction of Highway 224 at Ripplebrook, which is also where the Clackamas joins with a major tributary, the Oak Grove Fork. Highway 224 then follows the Clackamas River downstream for approximately 40 miles to the city of Clackamas.

For over twenty years the upper Clackamas had an exceptional hatchery summer steelhead run that long-time Northwest steelheaders fondly remember, and to this day they continue to cry in their beers over its loss (this author is one of them) (the publisher is another one). When wild fish populations continued

Rob Crandall with a nice Clackamas chromer. Photo by Robert Campbell

to struggle, ODFW decided to limit hatchery production to the lower river below the dams in order to minimize competition between wild and hatchery fish. No fish of hatchery origin are allowed to pass into the upper watershed, and the Clackamas River above the dams has been deemed a wild fish sanctuary. Fishing for salmon and steelhead is not allowed above Cazadero Dam.

The upper Clackamas generally flows crystal clear during the spring and summer months once run-off has subsided, but it can get dirty after a heavy rain. Trout fishing in the upper sections is surprisingly good for a west side stream. Both cutthroat and resident rainbow are present, as well as the occasional brook trout and brown trout. While some sections of the "Clack" are under catch-and-release regulations for trout, others allow for seasonal harvest at this time. Always check the regulations for the area you intend to fish, and remember that fishing regulations sometimes change from year to year.

Both cutthroat and rainbow average 6-10 inches in length on the upper Clackamas, though there are some much larger trout present. I have seen cutthroat up to 16-inches caught from the upper Clackamas, and a strain of rainbow that grows to several pounds. I have caught many of this type of rainbow from several Cascade west slope streams, including the Clackamas, Molalla and North Santiam. They are large, heavily-spotted trout that almost look like the famed Alaskan "leopard bows." Whether they are a unique strain, hybrid or other I am not sure, but they are present in small numbers and will make your angling year if you are

fortunate enough to encounter one. My friend Jeff Williams once caught one from the upper Clack that probably weighed around four-pounds, and it was one of the most striking trout that I ever laid eyes on. These fish are rare, so treat them gently and kindly release.

Bull trout are another rarity present in the upper Clackamas River, albeit in very small numbers. In recent years the United States Fish and Wildlife Service, in conjunction with the Oregon Department of Fish and Wildlife, has began a reintroduction program of bull trout to the Clackamas Basin. Bull trout had not been seen in the Clackamas since 1963. In 1999 they were listed as threatened under the Endangered Species Act.

In the summer of 2011, several dozen bull trout of varying life stages were translocated from the healthy Metolious River population to the Clackamas. Remarkably, some spawning of bull trout took place that fall in the Clack for the first time in 50 years! Bull trout are an apex predator and a missing link to a balanced system. They need cold, clean water in order to thrive. The upper Clackamas River above the dams is a wild, free-flowing river. It is a designated wild fish sanctuary. If bull trout have a chance at recovery anywhere, surely the upper Clackamas is a good place to start. It is illegal for anglers to target or retain bull trout, so if you are lucky to catch one, gently release it and consider yourself an important component of bull trout recovery.

In recent years the Oregon Sport Fishing Regulations book has featured a page that covers bull trout identification, since many anglers have a hard time distinguishing them from

Resources

Nearest cities/towns:
Oregon City, Clackamas, Carver, Barton, Estacada

Camping:
Clackamas River Ranger District
Mt. Hood National Forest
503-630-6861

Tackle:
The Fly Fishing Shop, Welches
www.flyfishusa.com

Fisherman's Marine and Outdoor
Oregon City
503 557-3313

Estacada Tackle
503-630-7424

Great American Tackle Shop
503-650-2662

Orvis
503-598-7680

Royal Treatment Fly Shop
503-850-4397

River City Fly Shop
503-579-5176

Visitor information:
Mt. Hood Area Chamber
www.mthood.org
503-622-3017

There are some impressive wild trout in the upper Clackamas, though they should always be handled with care and released to fight again another day. Photo by Robert Campbell

brook trout. The easiest way is by the dorsal fins. Brook trout have dark, worm-like markings on their dorsal fins; bull trout do not.

Bait fishing is prohibited on much of the upper Clackamas, though it never fails to surprise me how many "anglers" I observe plunking Power Bait in a sunny, foot-deep flat at one of the many campgrounds on the river. Speaking of camping, there are no less than 14 designated campgrounds on the Clackamas River between North Fork Reservoir and the confluence with the Collawash River. There are many more on tributaries and at the nearby Mt Hood Lakes, which makes the upper Clackamas an extremely popular area for camping during the summer months.

When fishing the upper Clackamas, it is important to note that much of the water is of the type not suitable for trout. Long, shallow flats without cover are not going to hold fish except in periods of low-light like early morning or evening, so don't target them during the day. Also, trout are not going to live in the middle of rapids or current that is too strong, it's just too difficult to eke out a living in such water and requires too much energy to do so. Look for softer pockets of water just off the main current, where a trout can conserve energy while the current brings it food. If such feeding lanes are shaded or

covered by overhanging brush, that's even better.

Riffles with a broken surface should also be targeted as this type of water is high in oxygen and tends to support good numbers of the aquatic insects that Clackamas trout like to eat, such as caddis, mayflies and stoneflies. The choppy surface also provides cover by making it harder for predators like kingfishers and osprey to detect the fish.

Fly fishermen will catch a bunch of nice trout by fishing the upper Clack when the water is shaded and the fish are less wary. Also use long, fine leaders tapering down to 6X as the trout—especially the larger ones—can be extremely weary in the ultra-clear water. Fluorocarbon tippets when nymphing are also a good idea. Have I mentioned I like SeaGuar brand fluorocarbon?

When the sun is off the water, dry fly fishing with Elk Hair Caddis, Trude Coachman and even Grasshopper patterns can be extremely effective on hungry trout. Insect populations here are not particularly robust, so the trout always seem to be hungry. Fly selection takes a back seat to reading the water and proper presentation. If you can manage a drag-free drift with either a dry fly or nymph, you'll be in business. There are several species of stonefly up here in addition to

the caddis, from tiny black stones up to the larger golden stones of mid-summer. Nymphing with a Prince Nymph or No. 8 Golden Stone can result in some banner days. Terrestrial patterns like ants and beetles are also very effective patterns on the upper Clackamas.

Gear fishermen will catch their share of trout here on small spoons and spinners. The venerable Rooster Tail spinner from Worden's is hard to beat in black, green or brown. Cast it into promising water, reel up any slack, and maintain just enough tension on the line to keep the spinner blade rotating as the lure swings across likely water. For best results the spinner blade should spin as slowly as possible in the current. I see far too many anglers err by starting to crank the reel like mad the second the lure hits the water, and the lure never gets down near the bottom where the fish are, while the blade spins faster than the fish like it. As a rule, reel only when necessary to maintain enough tension on the line to keep the blade spinning.

The upper Clackamas is a gorgeous mountain river that courses through some amazing country. There are dozens of smaller trout streams in the area that are just begging to be explored by the adventurous angler. The many trout lakes of the High Rocks area are also nearby, beckoning the hike-in angler who might savor the flavor of a brook trout frying in butter. Whether you visit this area to fish, hunt, camp, hike, swim, raft, kayak, birdwatch or photograph, you will instantly fall for the forested upper Clackamas and be glad to have such an amazing resource in your backyard.

If you love salmon and steelhead, then in the least you probably have mixed feelings about dams. As a native Oregonian, I often wonder what the Columbia River looked like when Lewis and Clark first saw it. I also wonder just how many salmon and steelhead used to course upstream prior to the river being mechanized. It also turns my stomach to realize that my own species so brazenly destroyed a super-race of Chinook salmon previously known as June Hogs by constructing Grand Coulee without fish passage. Dams aren't good for fish, and in many cases they're just plain lethal. Whenever I drive by the three Clackamas River dams on the mainstem near Estacada, Oregon, I always wonder what the true potential of such an awesome river must be without the structures that limit salmon and steelhead production, especially considering the incredible habitat that lays upstream just waiting to be exploited by salmonids.

The lower Clackamas River begins at the base of River Mill Dam, which by the way, generates enough electricity to power over 10,000 homes according to Portland General Electric. I tend to use electricity myself on a regular basis, so there you go—mixed feelings. PGE, by the way, spent a bazillion dollars to design and implement the world's longest operating fish ladder-- which was completed in 2006--in an attempt to improve passage of wild fish past the dams. Hopefully the 1.9 mile long conduit makes a difference.

The Clackamas emerges from Estacada Lake as a powerful, full-blown river. From there it charges another 23.5 miles before joining the Willamette River at Oregon City. In that 23.5 miles is some of the most popular and heavily-used salmon and steelhead water in the Pacific Northwest. Bank access on the lower Clackamas is spotty due to extensive private property, and for that reason the best river access is had by floating the river in a drift boat, or, running it in a jet sled.

Due to its size and flow, the lower Clackamas is a popular river for powerboats, that is, shallow-running, jet-powered craft that are designed for running white water rivers. However, once the river drops below 12 feet in height at the Estacada gauge, the river becomes unsafe for powerboats in several areas due to wide, shallow riffles. Though the Clackamas is

not really known as a difficult river to navigate, it is recommended that newcomers and beginners initially go with someone who knows the river, or, hire a guide. As with all Northwest rivers, the Clack is subject to constant change and dangerous conditions can occur overnight.

The lowest boat ramp on the Clackamas is at Clackamette Park in Oregon City, just upstream of the confluence with the Willamette River. This ramp provides power boaters with quick access to the popular Willamette River spring Chinook fishery below Willamette falls, as well as access to some good salmon and steelhead water on the lower reaches of the Clackamas River. Keep in mind that current angling regulations call for barbless hooks only when fishing below the 99E (McLoughlin Blvd.) bridge on the Clack.

There is decent bank access to the lowest reach of the Clackamas

at Clackamette Park on the south and Meldrum Bar Park on the north side of the river. Meldrum bar itself is a large gravel bar that extends out into the Willamette River just below the mouth of the Clackamas. This is a very popular area for plunkers targeting steelhead and spring Chinook headed to the Clack. Keep in mind that this section of the Willamette is tidally influenced, and at higher water levels the gravel bar can get submerged in a hurry by a rising tide. There is another popular plunking location right at the mouth of the Clackamas on the north side known as "The Blacktop," where fishing is often very good for salmon and steelhead, especially at high water.

There is also bank access to decent steelhead water at Cross Park in Gladstone just off of Arlington Street. Also off of Arlington is access to the "First Riffle," or "Bowling Alley Hole," thus named

Josiah Darr releases a wild steelhead. Photo by Josiah Darr

Kelly Reichner with a very fresh Clackamas winter steelhead caught on a Fisher Jig. They don't come any brighter than this one! Photo by Robert Campbell

because it is the first actual riffle on the river and a natural choke point for fish making their way upstream. The Gladstone Bowling Alley was also located nearby before being demolished. While salmon and steelhead do condense in this spot, so do snaggers. This location has a long history of attracting the wrong crowd who employ dubious techniques to "catch" fish. Garbage, foul language and fish hooked other than in the mouth are the rule here. In recent years local law enforcement has paid better attention to this location, but not enough. Undoubtedly not everyone who fishes The Bowling Alley is a snagger, but this is still the last place that I would take a kid fishing.

Riverside County Park is approximately three miles upstream from Clackamette and can be accessed via Evelyn Street off of Highway 212. The park features a very good boat ramp and bank access to fair water that traditionally has been very popular with plunkers at high water levels. This is not the very best salmon and steelhead water on the planet, but it is still salmon and steelhead water close to town, and an angler short on time could be here in a few minutes casting his/her troubles away.

Carver Park is the next access upstream and the most-used facility on the river, both for power boaters launching and drifters taking out after launching upstream at Barton. Some of the very best steelhead water on the river is located both upstream and downstream of here, which explains its popularity with boaters. Clear Creek, a tributary with wild runs of steelhead and coho, enters the Clackamas within the park. There is limited bank access here.

During the summer months the float from Barton to Carver is wildly popular with the splash-and-giggle crowd, and at times the scene at Carver became near-riotous as alcohol and crowded conditions did not mix. As things got worse, the County was forced to take action by banning alcohol in its parks. Not going far enough, the alcohol consumption, litter, nudity, trespassing and general malfeasance on the river continued until the County Commissioners approved an ordinance that allowed law enforcement officers to visually inspect park-goers' private property, i.e. coolers, bags, etc.

While summers are now somewhat tamer on the float from Barton to Carver, the river

still gets abused. If you choose the Clackamas as a place to make a float to cool off from the summer's heat, consider yourself forewarned.

Upstream, the expansive 116-acre Barton Park is also very popular with anglers.

This is the most popular launch on the river for drifters heading toward Carver and such hallowed salmon/steelhead venues as the Hippie Hole, Latourette's, Deep Creek Drift, Slab Hole, Grant's Park, the Dog Hole and the Beaver Dam Hole, among others. This series of long flats is classic steelhead holding water, and the fish tend to slow down and hang out here before moving on upriver, making them prime targets for an armada of power boat anglers who have adopted side-drifting as their method of choice, which is a technique well-suited to the Clack's longer flats.

Barton Park also provides the bank angler with some pretty good access to prime steelhead water. The runs both above and below the bridge at the park are very good holding water for coho and steelhead. There is more good water a short walk upstream from the boat ramp. Anglers may also park at a pull out on the other side of the river from the park to walk downstream to the popular Hippie Hole, which is tailor-made for swinging flies or hardware. Barton also features camping from May 1st through October 31st. All Clackamas County Parks on the river have day use fees, seasonal park hours, and varying facilities. For more information on the previously mentioned parks, including concise directions, visit www.clackamas.us/parks, or call the Parks Administration Office at (503) 742-4414.

Several miles upstream off Springwater Road is another put-in known as Feldheimer's. This is a rough, river rock and gravel ramp that is really only suitable for drift boats and rafts. The float from here down to Barton accesses some more good water, including the mouth of Eagle

Creek, a major tributary that hosts runs of steelhead, coho and spring Chinook. Bank anglers may access the mouth of Eagle Creek through Bonnie Lure State Recreation Area on the east side of the river.

Milo McIver State Park provides the upper-most access to boaters on the lower Clackamas, having two different ramps (upper and lower) within the park. The lower ramp is just a short distance above Feldheimer's, while the upper ramp is located just above one of the nastiest rapids on the lower river. This stretch of water is for experts only, so do not launch at the upper ramp if you don't have the proper experience, craft and know-how. A short distance below the first rapid is the Mine Field, an extremely technical piece of water that has destroyed many a boat over the years.

McIver Park, as locals call it, offers camping, hiking, horse trails, and of course, fishing. Some of the very best bank access on the entire lower river is at McIver Park, and the adventurous angler could spend a day exploring it all. The Clackamas Hatchery on Dog Creek is also located here, which is the final destination for many of the river's spring Chinook and winter steelhead, and all of its summer steelhead.

One of the best things about the lower Clackamas is the diversity of its fish runs, which provides a salmon and steelhead fishery year-round. Coho salmon are raised at Eagle Creek Fish Hatchery and provide a popular fishery during September and October. The first coho of the year usually enter the river without fail the last week of August, rain or not. I've often heard it said that the coho enter the Clack with the first fall rains, but this simply isn't the case. Certainly rain helps, but the Clackamas is a large river with ample flow for fish movement even at seasonally low levels. The fish come whether it rains or not.

The run continues to build with peak numbers present from mid-September to mid-October most years. Under current regulations, the Clackamas closes to Coho retention on October 31st to protect a late-arriving run of wild coho that are present in November and December. These spectacular, robust fish are mostly headed above the dams to spawn in the upper river, and they are generally larger than their hatchery counterparts. Only adipose fin-clipped coho, steelhead and Chinook may be retained at this time from the Clackamas.

Clackamas coho have a reputation for being extremely tight-lipped, and most years they are somewhat difficult to catch. Early in the run when the water is warmer, anglers generally use hardware to try and elicit a reactionary bite from fish that are just arriving to the river. Spinners in Chartreuse, purple, blue and pink are standard fare. In recent years, twitching jigs has accounted for its share of Clackamas River coho, with combinations of pink, purple and black being popular. Later in the run as the water cools, fishing with salmon roe gains effectiveness, and fishermen either suspend their bait below a float or drift-fish it depending on the water being fished. Early in the run, coho often amass just off the mouth of the Clackamas in the Willamette River, and can be caught by casting spinners, jigs or plugs either from a boat or off the bank.

The majority of the Clack's winter steelhead are raised at the Clackamas Hatchery at Dog Creek, though a small number are still reared and released at Eagle Creek. The Eagle Creek fish usually are the vanguard of the year's run, with fish sometimes showing in late November, but mid-December is more the norm. The bulk of the Clack's winter steelhead are comprised of wild brood stock that have somewhat spread the run out over the months, though there is still a natural tendency for the bulk of these fish to show up in late February or March just as their wild brethren do.

While side-drifting in power boats has largely taken over the winter steelhead scene on the Clackamas, there are still many anglers who prefer the slower pace of the drift boat. Initially there were many conflicts on the river as these two worlds collided, but things have mellowed some as both camps have come to realize that neither is going anywhere. Be advised that a bit of patience and a lot of river courtesy are advised while fishing the Clackamas. Although times have changed, in my book it is still bush-league and rude to cut-off other fishermen, fish right through a bank angler's

There are still remnant populations of searun cutthroat trout that return to tributaries of the lower Clackams, notably Deep Creek and Clear Creek. Photo by Robert Campbell

water, or otherwise act like you're the only boat on the river. There are times on the Clackamas when you wonder if anyone fishing there has ever even heard of the Golden Rule.

There is a tendency for bank anglers and drifters to demonize power boaters whether they deserve it or not. Perhaps this comes from a false assumption that they catch the bulk of the fish. Rest assured that is not the case, for Clackamas winter steelhead are caught on a variety of techniques from drift-fishing, to bobber and jig, hardware and fly. In fact, it is my opinion that these heavily-pressured fish often get turned off of the same old side-drifted presentation, and that something different is often what triggers a strike. I've seen many times where a group of anglers proficient with bobber and jigs came in behind side drifters and put on a clinic. On the Clackamas, the jig color combo of black, red and white, also known as "The Nightmare," is hard to beat.

Summer steelhead may show up in the Clackamas as early as February, but April, May and June are typically the best months. These chrome bullets are aggressive fish that will succumb to a variety of techniques. Summer steelhead are present in the river throughout the river all summer long, though the combination of low water and rowdy, high float traffic days is not a good recipe for successful angling. If you intend to target these fish during the dog days of summer, concentrate your efforts to the early morning or evening hours when traffic is minimal and the fish are less disturbed.

Spring Chinook typically begin to show up in the Clackamas as early as March, but numbers really start to build in April, May and June. Springer fishing holds up on the Clackamas as long as there is ample run-off to keep the river green and cool. As soon as the river begins to drop and clear, the springers don't bite as well. Clackamas spring Chinook like smaller plugs like Wiggle Warts, K-11 Kwikfish and Worden's Mag Lips. But most Clackamas Springers are caught on salmon roe, either back-bounced or fished under a float. Many of the fishing guides that I know will not fish for springers on the Clackamas without sand shrimp to compliment their eggs, so keep this in mind.

Spring Chinook are prized for their brute strength and oily flesh. They are without doubt one of the best tasting salmon on the planet. Though most anglers target them with bait, springers can be aggressive at times, and many a steelhead angler has been surprised by a spring Chinook hitting a jig, spinner or fly. Clackamas springers generally spend either two or three years in the ocean, with two-salt fish generally weighing 10-15 pounds, and three-salt fish weighing 15-25 pounds. Every year there are a few exceptional specimens that tip the scales to 30-pounds or more!

While the Clackamas River may not be the world's most pristine waterway, it is still a river with salmon, trout and steelhead in a populated region. Though I definitely prefer to fish a river with a quieter, more serene setting, I am also thankful to have a salmon and steelhead stream to fish so near to home when time is limited by work, soccer practice or gymnastics. Besides, the Clackamas is really like having two rivers in one, for the upper river is still pretty much intact, providing a great corridor of escape from the trappings of the modern world. And who knows, maybe someday there will no longer be the need for those dams on the Clackamas, and then we can see just how many salmon and steelhead it is capable of producing.

Mount Hood and the Sandy River, as seen from Sandy, Oregon. Photo by Rodney Smith

Collawash River

Origin ..... Confluence of East Fork Collawash River and Elk Lake Creek, just outside the eastern boundary of the Bull of the Woods Wilderness

Length .... ~12 miles

Regulations .... Artificial fly & lure only

Terminus   Upper Clackamas River about three miles south of Ripplebrook Ranger Station

Elevation at source .... ~2,300 feet

Elevation at mouth .... ~1,500 feet

Species: Wild rainbow, brook trout, and possibly bull trout

Best Methods: Very small, dark-colored spinners or fly fishing

Tips: The water here is extremely clear, use very light leader. SeaGuar fluorocarbon tippet material is advised when nymphing or throwing hardware.

The Collawash is a gorgeous mountain stream full of beautiful wild trout. Anglers will delight in an abundance of classic trout water. Photo by Robert Campbell

The Collawash River is a gorgeous mountain stream joining the upper Clackamas River approximately 35 miles southeast of Estacada. The Collawash, and its major tributary, the Hot Springs Fork, are healthy rivers with excellent habitat for native trout and salmonids. Both streams flow entirely within the Mt. Hood National Forest. The cold, clean water of the Collawash make this an excellent river to fish during the height of summer when other streams are suffering from warmer temperatures.

Access to the main Collawash is mostly excellent, though rugged, on the lower few miles as road # 63 begins at Two Rivers Campground and closely follows the river through a narrow gorge rimmed by jagged cliffs of columnar basalt. In a few places, massive basalt monoliths hang eerily over the roadway, leading one to think this would be a very bad place to be during an earthquake! Road 63 heads mostly south up the river, and access to the stream grows more difficult the further you go. Road #70 follows the Hot Springs Fork upstream to where it leaves the road near the trailhead to Bagby Hot Springs, another popular destination.

As you near Tom's Meadow, road #63 leaves the main Collawash for several miles and courses along a high ridgeline far above the river, though rumor has it that some adventurous anglers favor this stretch for its limited access and larger trout. If you do leave the road to scramble and forge your own trail to the river, remember that this is steep, remote country, and caution should be used to avoid injury or accident. It is advisable to always use the buddy system in wild places and don't take unnecessary risks. There is a rough trail that begins where the road leaves the river and follows its course into the gorge.

The Collawash flows clean, cold and pure, and the river's gradient is not as steep as one would think looking about the area. For these reasons, there are healthy populations of aquatic insects and plentiful habitat for the trout. Caddis, mayfly and stonefly populations are abundant, making this river tailor-made for fly fishing. While a box of bushy attractor flies and 3-5 weight rod rigged with a floating line are all you will need to catch your share of trout, having a box of imitative nymphs is recommended if you want to fool some of the larger fish here. A small black or brown Rooster Tail spinner is hard to beat for lure fishing.

In ideal water, the number of trout present is astounding. Don't be surprised if you pull a dozen or more small rainbows averaging 6-10 inches out of a single stretch of riffle water on this river. Quite often the trout are plainly visible, adding a dimension of excitement to the angling as you get to watch as they attack—or refuse—your fly. The water in this river is gin-clear and long, light tippets are advisable. Whenever fishing subsurface either with fly or lure, I always employ a fluorocarbon leader and the added expense is more than justified by the results. When dry fly fishing, never use a leader shorter than 10 feet for best results; 12-14 is better. Fluorocarbon is no good for dry fly fishing with small flies because it sinks.

While the vast majority of trout in both the main Collawash and Hot Springs Fork are typical mountain trout measuring on the small side, there are also some nice fish present. I once caught a gorgeous 17-inch fish a couple hundred yards below Pegleg Falls on the Hot Springs Fork. Heavily spotted and lacking parr marks like the smaller fish, this rainbow had a decidedly different look to it. There are some bigger trout here, but you will have to go through several dozen smaller fish to get to them. Bummer, eh? You can also target the larger fish by looking specifically for spots that appeal to bigger fish, that is, deeper, faster, rowdier water with slower feeding lanes to either side, especially if it is located in the shade or under overhanging brush. Bigger trout like adequate cover.

Both forks of the Collawash once had amazing runs of hatchery summer steelhead that provided an excellent fishery here and on the upper Clackamas. But those plants ceased long ago and regrettably a once-vibrant recreational fishery in a beautiful setting was ended. Today there remain wild runs of winter steelhead, spring chinook and coho salmon to both forks of the Collawash, though fishing for them is forbidden. The entire upper Clackamas watershed, in fact, is closed to salmon and steelhead fishing above Cazadero Dam, making the Collawash a catch-and-release trout fishery. That is, unless you catch a brook or brown trout. Under current regulations there is no size or limit on these species taken from the Clackamas or its tributaries above Cazadero. There are some brook trout in the upper reaches of the Collawash, but they are uncommon.

The area near the confluence of the main Collawash and Hot Springs Fork is a traditional wild spring chinook spawning area, and the clear water makes this a great place to come to watch these amazing fish do their thing in late summer or early fall. In the past there has been a poaching problem on spring chinook in this area, which is bizarre since the fish are well beyond decent table fare by the time they arrive this high in the system. But keep an eye out nonetheless, and report any suspicious activity in the area to law enforcement. It is up to the rest of us to protect these noble fish from those miscreants that would steal them from future generations.

Both forks of the Collawash River are also the ancestral home of one of our coolest native fish, the bull trout. There are rumors that a remnant population exists here, but targeting them is strictly off-limits. In recent years, the Oregon Department of Fish and Wildlife has begun a reintroduction program of bull trout into the upper Clackamas watershed in an attempt to fix a system out of balance and reverse past wrongs. The Collawash is excellent bull trout habitat, so don't be surprised if sometime in the future you hook into something much larger than a 14-inch rainbow on either of the forks. If you are so lucky, admire it, make a gentle release, and take pride that you have done your part in helping an amazing creature find a toe hold on its way to recovery.

Directions:

From Estacada, follow Highway 224 to Ripplebrook Ranger Station, then head south on road #46 to Two Rivers Campground, where the Collawash flows into the Clackamas. From here road #63 provides mostly good access for about nine miles until you reach Tom's Meadow, at which point best access is via fishermen's trails.

Resources

Nearest cities/towns:
Estacada

Tackle:
The Fly Fishing Shop, Welches
www.flyfishusa.com

Estacada Tackle
503-630-7424

Great American Tackle Shop
503-650-2662

Camping:
Clackamas River Ranger District
Mt. Hood National Forest
503-630-6861

Visitor information:
Mt. Hood Area Chamber
www.mthood.org
503-622-3017

It is our hope that anglers use this book as a starting point for their own adventures, like our own discovery of this waterfall and a creek full of trout on a tributary of the Hot Springs Fork of the Collawash River. Photo by Robert Campbell

Oak Grove Fork

Origin .....Northwest corner of Warm Springs Indian Reservation near Abbott Pass

Length.. ~21 miles

Regulations .... Artificial fly & lure only

Terminus ....Mainstem Clackamas River near Ripplebrook

Elevation at source .... ~3,700 feet

Elevation at mouth.................... ~1,300 feet

Species: Coastal cutthroat, brook, some rainbow and brown trout near the reservoirs

The Oak Grove Fork of the Clackamas River is a mountain stream of many personalities. From its headwaters within the Warm Springs Reservation, the Oak Grove Fork begins its journey as a tumbling little stream that flows through dense forest on its way to Clackamas Meadow. As it arrives near Clackamas Lake, the river transforms into a classic meadow stream, having the appearance of a spring creek from Montana or Wyoming.

The fly fishing along this stretch of the river is magical, with crystalline water and spooky trout challenging the angler. Here you will find mostly brook trout, though they aren't as easy to catch as often reported. Fishing the meadow stretch of the Oak Grove Fork is best done during the low-light periods of early morning or evening, as during the day the trout are hidden away in undercut banks or weed beds, not that you can't tempt them out with a crafty presentation. This is a lush environment and there are some surprisingly nice trout here for a mountain stream, though you'll have to use stealth techniques to connect with one. Expect brookies from this stretch to average 7-10 inches, with fish up to 15 inches available. There are a very few cutthroat in this stretch.

When fishing the meadow stretch, use long, light leaders and a quiet approach, and watch where your shadow falls. These trout are wary, and if they see your shadow or your fly line it could very well put them down. When dry fly fishing this stretch, it is advisable to cast down to the fish using John Judy's slack line technique to keep from casting over the fish with your fly line. In these calm waters you will have much better success using highly imitative caddis and mayfly patterns like the Hemingway Caddis or Comparaduns. This is no place for a No.10 yellow Humpy unless the sun has set. The meadow stretch is unique fishery for this part of the Cascade Mountains, so tread lightly, use existing trails, and please pick up any beer cans you see.

As the small river leaves Clackamas Meadow, it

The meadow stretch of the Oak Grove Fork provides challenging angling for cagey trout in a spring creek setting. Long, fine leaders are recommended along with stealth tactics. Please tread lightly. Photo by Robert Campbell

picks up speed on the way to Timothy Lake. Cutthroat become more common in this wooded gorge, and the river varies here from plunge pools to classic riffle water. The trout are more willing in this section, as there is a lot of shade and better hidey holes than in the meadow stretch. Still, stealth is required to fool the largest fish, and there are a few brookies and cutts here between 12-14 inches, nice-sized for mountain trout.

From Clackamas Meadow, the Pacific Crest Trail follows the Oak Grove Fork on the north side all the way to Timothy Lake, while trail No. 534 follows the south bank of the river to Timothy. Pick up the PCT near Joe Graham Horse Camp at the meadow. You can jump on trail No. 534 at Clackamas Lake Campground, or, where it crosses road No. 57 west of the campground. While both trails follow the stream, it's still somewhat of a scramble to get down to the water in most places.

As the Oak Grove Fork leaves Timothy Lake, it has more than doubled in size from all of the tributaries and seeps that flow into the lake. Below Timothy the river is deceptively powerful as it tumbles through a deep gorge. Wading in the first few miles below the dam is dangerous, do not fall into the river! The access here is difficult at best, and care must be taken to avoid an accident. This is no place to fish alone.

This gorge section, however, is home to some of the most beautiful native cutthroat you will ever set your eyes on, and angling pressure is minimal. The trout are heavily spotted and have striking coloration. Picture fish. This stretch of river is well-suited to the adventurous angler who is physically fit and has wilderness experience. The trout here are numerous and competitive, and you will be surprised how many might be crammed into ideal water. The fish are not picky, and bushy, high-floating attractors are a good choice for dry flies. Just about any nymph size 12 or smaller should do fine. I prefer a No. 14 Prince Nymph as the white biot wings seem to show up well in shadowed water and dark pools.

The Oak Grove Fork below Lake Harriet has challenging access, but you can bushwhack up from the lake through this jungle, or, access the river where road No.46 crosses it near Ripplebrook Campground. From there you can hike, scramble and wade up or downstream, though this type of fishing is not for the meek.

Directions

To fish the upper river above Timothy or the meadow stretch, take Highway 26 east from Government Camp about 11 miles to Skyline Road. Follow Skyline Road roughly 9 miles to Clackamas Lake Ranger Station. From here you can fish the meadow stretch up or downstream, or you can follow the river to Timothy Lake via the previously mentioned trails. Also, you can access the lower end of these trails from the Oak Grove Fork Campground at Timothy Lake. From the boat ramp there is a shoreline trail that leads to the inlet of the river and the trails, which by the way, is a very productive area of the lake. The lower river can be reached via Road No. 57 below Timothy, which follows the river nearly to its the mouth.

Resources

Nearest cities/towns:
Rhododendron, Zigzag, Government Camp, Estacada

Camping:
Clackamas River Ranger District
Mt. Hood National Forest
503-630-6861

Tackle:
The Fly Fishing Shop, Welches

Fisherman's Marine and Outdoor
Oregon City
503 557-3313

Visitor information:
Mt. Hood Area Chamber
www.mthood.org
503-622-3017

Sed ut perspiciatis unde omnis iste natus error sit voluptatem.
Photo by Robert Campbell

Sandy River

Length... ~56 miles

Origin .... Reid Glacier on the west slope of Mt. Hood.

Terminus   Flows into the Columbia River near the town of Troutdale, Oregon

Elevation at source .... around 6,000 feet

Elevation at mouth........................ ~10 feet
The river drops over 4,500 feet in its first 13 miles.

Species: Spring & fall chinook, coho, winter & summer steelhead, a sparse population of resident rainbow and cutthroat trout, whitefish. Smelt, shad and white sturgeon are occasional visitors.

Best Methods: Varies widely by species.

Tips: The Sandy fishes best at river levels from 9-11 feet.

The Sandy River is one of the most beautiful salmon and steelhead streams on the planet, making it hard to believe that it's located only a few miles from Oregon's largest city. Photo by Robert Campbell

Born high on Mount Hood, the Sandy River has been shaped by fire and ice. Glaciers once scoured the Sandy valley making it wider and deeper. Numerous eruptive periods, with the most recent occurring just 200 or so years ago, have shaped the landscape and helped carve the dramatic canyon through which the river flows.

Mud flows and pyroclastic events during the Old Maid eruptive period charged down the mountain and into the Sandy River gorge, resulting in lahar inundations that buried old growth forest and altered the landscape for decades. In recent years, erosion has cut into these silty deposits, once again exposing long-buried "ghost forests" of ancient trees for all to see. One of these is located at Oxbow Park just upstream of the boat launch, another downstream near the Greek Camp.

When Lewis and Clark ventured near the mouth of the river in 1805, they named it the Quicksand River because of the "emence quantitys" of ashy, silty sand located there. Little did they know that their arrival to the area followed over a decade of volcanic activity on the mountain, activity that flushed a huge sediment load down river to the delta. At some point in subsequent years the name was shortened to the Sandy. In recent years, sulphur releases high on the mountain remind us that Mt Hood the stratovolcano is only sleeping, not extinct.

The Sandy River is beautiful. As a salmon and steelhead-bearing river located on the fringe of Oregon's most densely populated region, the Sandy is remarkably unique. Where other urban rivers have been dammed, logged and polluted into oblivion, the Sandy continues to hold on as a spawning destination for runs of Chinook, Coho and steelhead despite the injuries inflicted upon it by mankind. Today, the Sandy is a river on the mend, and the short-term side effects of dam removal will gradually lead to a more natural state.

Marmot Dam on the mainstem, and Little Sandy River Dam on the tributary of the same name, were built early in the 20th Century as key components of the Bull Run Hydroelectric Project. The project was a convoluted system of diversion dams, canals and flumes that sent water to Roslyn Lake to feed a powerhouse on the Bull Run River. Like so many other ill-conceived projects of its time, the Bull Run Hydro Project gave little consideration to the long-term effects on the river and its wildlife. This re-plumbing of the Sandy's natural flow and alteration of its chemical signature played havoc on fish runs.

In light of this and other environmental concerns, the dams were removed in 2007 and 2008, and the entire hydro system was decommissioned, once again opening up crucial miles of vital habitat for the Sandy's wild fish runs, and, returning the water to the river below Marmot. At the time of Marmot's removal, it was estimated that a sediment load of at least 900,000 cubic yards of material had been trapped and stored by the dam. While in the short term no one is quite sure what effect the flushing of this unnatural build-up will have, most agree that as the river returns to a more natural state that fish runs will respond favorably to the removal of the dams. Many believe that they already have.

The Sandy River is a blessing for Metro area anglers, as well as a destination fishery for those who love to fish for salmon and steelhead. With a wide array of salmonid species returning to the Sandy at various points on the calendar, the Sandy is a year-round fishery. It's proximity to town makes it possible for an angler to get from an office desk to a steelhead riffle in less than an hour, and, what's not to love about that?

It never fails to amaze me how wild and scenic the Sandy River canyon is, especially considering its nearness to downtown Portland's skyscrapers. Much of the canyon has been preserved in a natural state, with massive Douglas fir and western red cedar looming over the landscape. The canyon is lush, with water-loving plants like maidenhair fern, devil's club, salmonberry and trillium common in season. To drop into the Sandy River canyon is to leave the modern world behind. You might even get the feeling that you're in Alaska instead of bustling western Oregon.

The Sandy has a diversity of anadromous fish. First slowly, and now more rapidly, we are learning from yesterday's environmental crimes and trying to put the pieces back together. All wild fish in the Sandy are now protected under catch-and-release regulations—anglers are not allowed to harvest Chinook, coho or steelhead

unless they are marked as hatchery origin with an adipose fin clip. This is as it should be. There is also a heightened awareness of the importance of both hatchery and wild fish, and most anglers enjoy having the option of harvesting hatchery fish while gently releasing wild fish and therefore playing a part in their recovery.

And in recent years wild fish seem to be responding. Wild Fall Chinook runs have been robust in the lower river. The faulty hatchery practices of yesterday have been vastly improved and now only in-basin stocks are used to propagate hatchery steelhead. The wild broodstock steelhead program has been wildly successful and popular. Many Sandy River old-timers comment that there seem to be more wild winter steelhead in the Sandy than they have seen in decades, if ever. With such a variety of fish occupying the calendar, the Sandy promises a salmon and steelhead fishery 365 days a year, provided the river is in shape.

Fall Chinook start to show up in the lower Sandy River near the end of August, and the run builds through September and begins to fade in mid-October. Most fall Chinook in the Sandy are of wild origin, though occasionally a fin-clipped fish is caught, most likely a stray from a different Columbia River stock. Many anglers choose not to intentionally target the Chinook because of this, and instead enjoy the occasional tussle with the king of salmon while targeting hatchery coho. Fall Chinook in the Sandy typically inhabit the lower river, with numbers particularly thick from Oxbow down. Several upper tributaries have remnant runs, however, at this time salmon and

Resources

Nearest cities/towns:
Sandy, Troutdale

Accommodations:
Mount Hood Village

Tackle:
The Fly Fishing Shop, Welches
www.flyfishusa.com

Fisherman's Marine and Outdoor
Oregon City
503 557-3313

Estacada Tackle
503-630-7424

Great American Tackle Shop
503-650-2662

Orvis
503-598-7680

Royal Treatment Fly Shop
503-850-4397

River City Fly Shop
503-579-5176

Fisherman's Marine and Outdoor
Delta Park
503 283-0044

Visitor information:
Mt. Hood Area Chamber
www.mthood.org
503-622-3017

steelhead fishing is closed on the Sandy above the mouth of the Salmon River.

From mid-September through the end of October and into November, the Sandy's fall Chinook put on quite a show as they move onto shallow gravel bars in order to spawn. It's a pleasure just to watch as these powerful fish fight, thrash and dig their redds in the shallows. There are several popular viewing areas at Oxbow Regional Park where the salmon spawn year after year, and these areas are closed to angling in order to protect the fish.

For over thirty years there has been an annual Salmon Festival at Oxbow Park, usually the second or third week in October when spawning activity is at its peak. The festival celebrates over six million years of salmon returning to the Sandy, and participants strive to educate and promote the importance of salmon to the Pacific Northwest landscape. Habitat and healthy watersheds are the focus. More progress.

Wild coho salmon were once so rare in the Sandy that you threw a party if you caught one, not so any more. While coho numbers are always oddly subject to periods of boom or bust, numbers in the Sandy have increased markedly since the grim years of the late 80's and 90's. Hatchery coho are reared at the Cedar Creek hatchery off Ten Eyck Road near the town of Sandy, and these fish provide a popular sport fishery each fall from the mouth of the river up to the

hatchery. Angling pressure increases dramatically the closer one fishes to the hatchery.

Sandy river silvers are like coho everywhere else, that is, they can either be freakishly aggressive and easy to catch, or, extremely moody and impossible to catch. Because the river is usually at seasonal low flows about the time the coho run gets going, anglers can sometimes be faced with tough conditions if the water is clear. That's why seasoned Sandy River coho anglers always hope for the Sandy to have a bit glacial "murk" to it during coho season.

Being glacial in origin, the Sandy picks up rock flour and transports it down river. Rock flour is nothing more than suspended particulates that originate under the crushing forces of glaciers as they compress and grind the rock beneath them. During the summer and fall months, it is common for the Sandy to flow with some opacity to its color, that is, with a greenish-gray color that is caused by the presence of rock flour that has been released as glacial ice melts off, or, as rain washes it into the system. As long as the water does not become too turbid, Sandy River coho usually bite best when the river has a bit of this "glacial" color to it in the fall.

When Sandy River coho are on the snap, anglers enjoy catching them on hardware like spinners and spoons. The No. 4 Blue Fox Vibrax in chartreuse, pink or blue is an all-time favorite spinner, and the

Acme Little Cleo, B.C. Steel and P-Line Pro Steel are popular spoons. Avoid using hardware when the river is extremely clear unless you are fishing at first or last light, or in pocket water with a rowdy, broken surface. Hardware thrown near to a skittish school of silvers in low, clear water usually only serves to scatter the herd. In this situation it is better to stealthily float fish with eggs or jigs.

In my younger years I spent a **lot** of time fly fishing for silvers on the Sandy in the pocket water below Cedar Creek with Jason Hambly of Lamiglas rods, and we caught our share of fish.

Every year it seemed that the fish wanted a different color and pattern of fly, so each fall we had to go through our boxes to find the right offering. One year it was a Purple Dredger; the next, a three-inch long black bunny leech; and during one year with cold nights, little rain and extremely clear water, all we could get them on was a pink Glo Bug. The fish always bit best on a dead-drifted fly, although occasionally we would get one on the swing at the end of the drift.

Winter steelhead are the signature fish of the Sandy River Basin. The Sandy's wild winter steelhead are an impressive, robust breed of fish. They are special indeed. Winter steelhead have been caught from the Sandy as early as November, but the run really doesn't get going until December and really shines in January, February and March. Sandy River winter steelhead average between 6 and 10 pounds, though larger specimens—sometimes much larger— are often encountered. Each season the Sandy sees its share of twenty-plus pound specimens, and it's my personal belief that the Sandy is vastly underrated as a trophy steelhead stream.

As Mark Bachmann points out, there are probably several different strains of steelhead returning to the Sandy, each with its own unique characteristics that were shaped over time by different areas of the river and/or tributaries. Mark is the owner and proprietor of The Fly Fishing Shop in Wemme, a village up on the mountain by which the Sandy River flows. The Fly Fishing Shop is one of the most complete fly shops anywhere, as Mark has tailored his selection to both the local as well as the travelling angler. Any serious fly angler visiting the Mt Hood Country should definitely pay him a visit.

In addition to excellent numbers of wild winter steelhead, the Sandy also has a return of wild broodstock hatchery fish. This is a relatively new hatchery practice where wild fish are used as broodstock to propagate offspring that are fin-clipped and available for angler harvest. Because in-basin stocks are used, the "genetic pollution" and associated effects on wild fish are mitigated. Wild fish are provided a further buffer from anglers and there are still some fish available for fishermen to take home, kind of the best of both worlds.

Wild or hatchery, Sandy River steelhead can be crazy-aggressive when conditions are right. Their affinity for smashing the swung lure or fly makes them popular with fly anglers and hardware fishermen alike. When the river is in prime shape with good visibility, there is nothing like the vicious grab from an angry steelhead on a spoon or fly.

Of course, this inherent aggressiveness also makes the Sandy's winter steelhead susceptible to a wide variety of techniques, including fly fishing, drift fishing, float and jig, casting hardware, pulling plugs and more. Most conscientious anglers refrain from using diver-and-bait when targeting the Sandy's

steelhead because the fish are often hooked deep and mortality increases. It makes no sense to kill wild fish that you can't legally keep.

Many Northwest rivers are known for having a signature color that works particularly well on its fish, and the Sandy is no different. On the Sandy, it's pink. Whether fishing with plugs, jigs, flies or other, Sandy River steelhead love pink. That's why fishing with pink worms in Oregon first took root on the Sandy. The fish gobble them up like candy! They particularly like the four-inch steelhead worms from Mad River Manufacturing. If I were to send a novice out on the Sandy on a mission to catch his/her first steelhead, I would rig them up with a pink worm on an 1/8 oz jig head fished under a float. This rig will cover a lot of water in a hurry, and Sandy River steelhead love a pink worm!

In addition to winter steelhead, the Sandy still receives a meager plant of hatchery summer steelhead. These fish begin to show up in March and are available until the river becomes too turbid to fish in mid-summer. Though not nearly as plentiful as the winter steelhead, Sandy summer steelhead are quality fish that provide angling opportunity from late winter clear into fall.

I remember it like it was yesterday, the first summer steelhead I ever caught came from the Sandy River. The year was 1979. I was ten-years-old. As we pulled into the top of the Big Bend Hole on the lower river, I cocked my rod and looked to my dad for permission. Once the boat was anchored he gave me the nod. First cast with a No. 6 pearl-pink Corky rig, no yarn or bait on it, just the Corky. "Is the Corky too big?" I had asked.

"No," replied Dad, "It's big, but not too big… they'll hit it." And boy, did he! First cast, tighten up on the slack, tap, tap on the bottom, then TAP, TAP as my first summer steelhead hit. I set the hook as much as the whippy Eagle Claw fiberglass rod let you back then, and it was but a split second before that fish flew out of the water like a missile, trying to punch a hole in the sky! For so many of us from the Portland area, the Sandy is a river full of memories as well as fish.

The spring Chinook run on the Sandy is also comprised of both wild and hatchery fish. Sandy River springers begin to show up in April, but in most years the fishing doesn't really take off until late May and June. The spring Chinook run timing on the Sandy extends well beyond that of other area streams, with the fishing often holding up through much of July. Whether this is due to the cooler water or genetics is uncertain, but it is possible to catch a quality springer out of the Sandy for over a third of the calendar year! While bobber-fishing or back-bouncing roe is the preferred method for targeting springers, the Sandy's spring Chinook can be extremely aggressive and may be caught on spinner and spoons, and even flies.

Robert Campbell with a robust hatchery fish that slammed a Mad River Steelhead Worm. Photo by Robert Campbell

There are some resident rainbow and cutthroat trout in the Sandy, especially near the mouths of tributaries, but populations are so low that you'd be better off targeting trout in one of the many smaller streams that flow into the Sandy like the Zigzag or Salmon Rivers, which are covered by different chapters in this book.

Although there is a lot of private property on the Sandy both on the lower river and in the vicinity of the town of Sandy, anglers have mostly unfettered access to the river thanks to a 2002 decision by the Oregon Land Board that deemed the Sandy a navigable waterway. This designation basically means that the state owns both the bed and banks of the river up to the normal high water mark as ceded by the Federal Government at the inception of statehood. While there has been some contention (mostly by property owners) as to what exactly the high water mark is, most agencies have come to agree that this is the point at which permanent vegetation takes root. With the state having ownership of the bank up to this point, anglers are allowed complete access to the river.

Obviously, this decision resulted in some very irate property owners who were dismayed by the language in their deeds stating that they owned both the bank and bed of the river, and rightfully so. How would you like to purchase your own little slice of heaven only to find out later that the state considers it a highway of sorts? While the angst of landowners is understandable to a point, it is also ridiculous to claim that you "own" a river, and public access to our waterways is mostly a good thing—especially for fishermen. If only we could get the small percentage of people who litter, vandalize and behave as miscreants to care for such places like the rest of us do.

There are two popular floats on the river. The first, from Oxbow Regional Park to Dabney State Park, is roughly six miles and covers some of the best holding water on the river. The water varies from long, promising flats to classic riffles to broad tailouts. There are even a few stretches of pocket-water and some deep, swirling Chinook holes. Boaters with intermediate to good skills should have little trouble on this stretch, though log jams, sweepers and other hazards are always a possibility, so even experienced river boatmen need to exercise caution at all times. Only suitable river craft like drift boats, rafts and pontoon boats should be used. It is advisable to always check for recent river conditions at a reputable sporting goods store like Fisherman's Marine and Outdoor before heading out. Be advised that Oxbow and Dabney Parks are managed by different agencies, so there is a day-use fee at each.

The float from Dabney Park down to Lewis and Clark State Park in Troutdale is approximately three miles and is also a relatively tame float, but once again, caution should always be exercised when boating on moving water. Power boats become more common on the lower river, though experienced skippers will run all the way up to the power boating deadline at Dabney State Park when the river levels allow. It is unlawful to fish out of a boat upstream from a point that is 200 feet below the Oxbow Park boat ramp.

There is excellent bank access to the Sandy at Dodge Park, Cedar Creek Hatchery, Oxbow Park and Dabney Park. There is another float from Dodge Park down to Oxbow, but this is extremely dangerous water and should only be attempted by experts. Many boats have been sunk on this stretch of river, even by experienced boatmen. The water up there is extremely technical and there is virtually no room for error.

The Sandy River is one of Oregon's treasures. It is without doubt one of the prettiest rivers on the planet, as well as a place that is near and dear to the hearts of many Northwest sportsmen and women. So love the Sandy and its magnificent steelhead. Treat the wild fish with care. Enjoy the hatchery fish with asparagus and a glass of Pinot. Take your children there to watch wild salmon spawn in the shadow of skyscrapers and to show them that we *can* have it both ways. Clean up someone else's garbage and vote for politicians who think that clean water and wild places are important, no, essential. And maybe, just maybe, the Sandy River will be just as beautiful and just as promising when your own son or daughter is ready to catch his or her first steelhead.

Ten-year-old Claire Brown with a couple of nice silvers from the Sandy. Photo by Rodney Smith

Salmon River

Length.. ~12 miles

Regulations .... Artificial fly & lure
Catch & Release
Closed to bait, steelhead and salmon fishing

Terminus   Joins the Upper Sandy River
near the town of Zigzag

Elevation at source ....over 7,000 feet

Elevation at mouth..................... 1,370 feet

Species: Coastal cutthroat trout

Best Methods: Fly or lure.

Tips: Wait for seasonal snowmelt to substantially subside before attempting to fish this brawling little river, usually around the beginning of July.

Cold, clean and pure, one has to wonder why there aren't more salmon in the Salmon River.
Photo by Robert Campbell

The Salmon River begins high on Mt. Hood near the base of Palmer Glacier where it carries snow melt on its way to the Sandy River. Much like the Zigzag River, the Salmon begins life in a free fall as it cascades down the slopes of Mt Hood toward easier terrain. The Salmon doesn't really become fishable until it levels off a bit in a stretch that parallels Highway 26 east and south of Trillium Lake. The river here can be accessed via fishermen's trails, but the cutthroat up here lead a brutal existence and are tiny. South of Trillium Lake, Forest Roads lead to trails that access the upper river where few people fish. You'll need a good map.

The Salmon River once hosted robust runs of steelhead, chinook and coho, but those runs are but a remnant of what they once were. At this time, there is no salmon or steelhead fishing allowed on the Salmon River, but that is subject to change as it has in recent years. However, the Salmon does have a fantastic population of cutthroat trout available for catch-and-release angling, and this is an excellent mountain stream to fish during the heat of the summer.

The best angler access to the Salmon is from the lower end. The Wildwood Recreation Site, managed by the Bureau of Land Management, is a great place to begin. Wildwood is located approximately 40 miles east of Portland on Highway 26. The access road is located on the south side of the highway near mile marker 39. Wildwood is a 550-acre forested park featuring the unique Cascade Streamwatch, a subterranean viewing window built right into the bed of a small tributary of the Salmon River. The creek is a rearing area for juvenile salmon and steelhead as well as the home of cutthroat trout, which you may view

through the window and get a trout's-eye view of a mysterious underwater world.

Wildwood also has 2.5 miles of paved trails winding through a beautiful mixed forest of Douglas fir, western red cedar, big leaf maple, vine maple, grand fir and cottonwood trees. The Wetland Boardwalk interpretive trails venture through a marsh that is a magnet for wildlife. Birders will love this area for the excellent variety of species. Once, in less than ten minutes, I saw a Goshawk, yellow warblers, brown creeper, pileated woodpecker, wood ducks, Steller's Jays, Common Yellowthroat and more. Blacktail deer are plentiful in this area, as are black bear. The trails also provide excellent access points to the river.

There are good maps of the area available for free at kiosks in the park, but there is a nominal day use fee to use the area. Wildwood also features abundant picnic areas, plentiful well-kept restrooms, ball fields, a playground and easy access to nearby services in the towns of Wemme, Welches and Zigzag. And why is all of this relevant to the angler? Because Wildwood is an excellent family facility located reasonably close to town where the kids can go Sasquatch ape-crazy in the woods interacting with nature while you sneak up on some trout!

A few miles east of Wildwood on Highway 26 in Zigzag, turn south onto Salmon River Road to reach several more miles of excellent river access. About 2.6

miles from Highway 26 is the trailhead to the Old Salmon River Trail No. 742A, which follows the river upstream 2.2 miles. This is an easy trail that leads to some excellent riffle and pocket water holding plentiful trout. Green Canyons Campground is about 4.5 miles up River Road from Highway 26.

Like most mountain rivers, the trout here are on the small size (6-12 inches), but they are many. They are also fairly easy targets on small spinners like the Rooster Tail, Mepps Aglia and Blue Fox. For flies all you will need most of the time are bushy, high-floating attractors like Stimulators, Humpies or Wulffs. I once fished here all day with a No. 14 brown Elk Hair Caddis without changing my fly. There are plentiful caddis in the Salmon River, as well as a good yellow stonefly hatch in June and July, followed by a strong emergence of October caddis in Autumn. You will marvel at the size of some of the Douglas fir and red cedar along this trail.

Trail No. 742A ends at the downstream side of a bridge on River Road. On the upstream side of the road, Trail No. 742, The Salmon River Trail, begins. This is by far my favorite stretch of the river. Trail No. 742 starts with a rapid climb uphill away from the river on a narrow path that has treacherous cliffs on the right. Watch your footing, and keep pets and young children on a very short leash. The trail here is not particularly dangerous, that is, unless you leave it. After a quarter-mile or so, the trail regains the river and a lovely walk through an incredible temperate rainforest ensues. The hiking is so pleasant that you just might forget about the fishing. This is a lush area and very beautiful. Watch out for spiny devil's club as it is widespread, especially in the small ravines and creek beds that lead to the river. Beautiful maidenhair fern is also common.

For the first couple of miles, the trail follows the river closely in most places. There are a handful of "easy" access points in this stretch, and many more that are a bit of a scramble. But this is a quality angling experience in a gorgeous setting, and the trout are wild and plentiful. While mostly small, there are a few 12-16 inch cutthroat in this stretch that will really bend that three-weight. For whatever reason, the trout in the Salmon River are scrappy fish that fight above their weight class. Occasionally you will spot some wild spring Chinook lazing in the deeper holes, or a steelhead in a riffle, but they are off limits to angling.

A couple of miles in on trail No. 742 you will reach a Forest Service check

Resources

Nearest cities/towns:
Rhododendron, Zigzag, Government Camp

Accommodations:
Mount Hood Village

Tackle:
The Fly Fishing Shop, Welches

Visitor information:
Mt. Hood Area Chamber
www.mthood.org
503-622-3017

The Salmon River's wild trout are scrappy fish that fight like hell for their size. Photo by Robert Campbell

Warning: wild trout ahead! Photo by Robert Campbell

point where you are required to fill out a free permit which you must carry on your person as the trail ventures into the Salmon-Huckleberry Wilderness. Shortly after this point the trail leaves the river and traverses a high ridge for several miles before dropping back to the river. Fit, aggressive hikers can explore this upper stretch of river on a day hike, while others may want to backpack and camp. At the time of this writing, you are allowed to catch and retain two cutthroat trout on the upper Salmon River above Final Falls, 8-inch minimum length. Also, there is currently no size or limit on the number of brook trout taken, though you should always check the most recent regulations before heading out.

Like so many other streams in the Mt. Hood Forest, the Salmon's water runs ultra-clear after the spring run-off has subsided. This makes for some tricky wading as the water is often much deeper than it appears. Be careful. The clear water is both blessing and curse. While it allows you to often see the fish and observe their behaviors, it also allows them to see you, so fluorocarbon leaders and stealth tactics are advised in order to connect with the biggest trout. And remember, fluorocarbon sinks, so only use it when fishing subsurface techniques, not while dry fly fishing.

Sunrise over Mount Hood is best seen headed west on Highway 26 with a cup of coffee in one hand, the steering wheel in the other and fly rods strapped to the top. Photo by Rodney Smith

Zigzag River

Length................................~12 miles

Origin....................Zigzag Glacier, Southwest flank of Mt. Hood

Terminus.........Joins the Upper Sandy River near the town of Zigzag

Elevation at source...........over 7,000 feet

Elevation at mouth.....................1,375 feet

Species: Coastal cutthroat trout

Best Methods: Fly or lure. Closed to bait, steelhead and salmon fishing.

Tips: Wait for seasonal snowmelt to substantially subside before attempting to fish this brawling little river, usually around the beginning of July.

The topography of the Zigzag River is not what one typically expects of a quality trout stream. The river literally falls off of Mount Hood on its quick march to the Sandy River. The extreme upper stretches are virtually unfishable due to the lack of any type of conceivable holding water that could harbor a trout.

You may reach an upper stretch of the river via Kiwanis Camp Road #2639, but you'd be better off focusing your attention a bit further downriver where the grade softens a bit and the habitat is more suitable for the river's coastal cutthroat trout. At the end of this road just a few miles off Highway 26 is the trailhead to Little Zigzag falls, a gorgeous 75-foot cataract located in old-growth forest at the end of an easy 10 minute walk. It is a pleasure to sit in the mist of these falls during the heat of a summer day.

The Zigzag is a rowdy little stream, but the trout are there, tucked into small areas of relief out of the main flow where the scouring current may deliver to them a diet of small stoneflies, caddis and terrestrial insects. The trout in this river aren't huge, limited in size by the raucous environment, short season and scarcity of food. But they are wild and beautiful, and any angler who enjoys a challenge will welcome that posed by this tumbling mountain stream. Expect to catch cutthroat mostly in the 6-10 inch range, though occasionally you may be surprised by fish of a foot-long or more.

The fish are not overly selective, and this is a great

The trout in this river, coastal cutts, aren't big but they are wild and beautiful. This is a great stream for dapping attractor flies or dead-drifting dark-colored beadhead nymphs. Photo by Merrilee Lewis

little river for dapping bushy attractor flies like Wulff's and Coachman's in pockets behind boulders for eager trout. Small, dark-colored nymphs like the Prince or a black Pheasant Tail are excellent for imitating the river's little black stoneflies. Spinners like the Worden's Rooster Tail or the Panther Martin are great for probing the plentiful pocket water on this stream.

The Zigzag is a sanctuary stream for spawning wild chinook and steelhead, so please handle all fish gently before returning them to the water. That 10-inch "rainbow" that you carefully release today may very well return to the Sandy River Watershed in a few years as a robust winter steelhead weighing between ten and twenty pounds!

At this time, the Zigzag is closed to salmon and steelhead fishing and is catch-and-release only for trout—no bait allowed. If you are fortunate to see salmon or steelhead spawning in the Zigzag, please enjoy the sight and leave them be, and relish the fact that we still have pockets where wild fish are left alone to do their thing.

Access to the river is somewhat challenging due to both the rugged terrain and private property. For those reasons, I like the stretch in the area around Tollgate Campground, just a couple miles east of the town of Zigzag. The campground gets its name because the last tollgate on the Barlow Toll Road was located here from 1846-1919. The Pioneer Bridle Trail #766 parallels the river here for approximately a mile before the Zigzag crosses back to the north side of Highway 26. The area around the confluence with Still Creek also provides decent angling despite the noise from the highway, and some of the biggest trout are caught in this stretch.

From the town of Zigzag to the mouth, access is hampered by extensive private property, but a polite inquiry may find you pleasantly angling for mountain trout in a new friend's backyard. In town you may access the river at the end of Road 9 where it dead ends. You may also get to some good trout water by parking behind the restaurant on Woodlands Drive and accessing a fisherman's trail along the river.

Directions

Head east on Highway 26 approximately 42 miles from Portland to town of Zigzag. The lower 5-6 miles of river hold the best habitat and therefore the most trout.

The short trek into Little Zigzag falls makes a great introductory hike for youngsters. Photo by Robert Campbell

Resources

Nearest cities/towns:
Rhododendron, Zigzag, Government Camp

Accommodations:
Mount Hood Village

Tackle:
The Fly Fishing Shop, Welches
www.flyfishusa.com

Visitor information:
Mt. Hood Area Chamber
www.mthood.org
503-622-3017

The Zigzag River offers refuge from the summer heat as well as excellent dry fly fishing. Photo by Robert Campbell

Camp Creek

Length.. 7 miles

Regulations .... Artificial fly & lure
Catch & Release

Difficulty .... Moderate

Elevation at source .... 3,500 feet

Elevation at mouth..................... 2,000 feet

Species: Cutthroat, rainbow trout

Best Methods: Fly fishing

Tips: Fish beadhead nymphs, wets or dries

West of the Summit, all the way to the town of Sandy, Highway 26 follows the route of the old Barlow Road, which in its day was the most important development in the settling of Oregon.

One of the most treacherous passages of the trail was Laurel Hill. Here, the pioneers had to rope their wagons to trees to let them down the slope. Many wagons were lost on this slope and the scars left by the wagons can still be seen in the slide. The spot is marked by a sign along the highway and the trail to Laurel Hill is short. Hike out to Laurel Hill then imagine the relief of a pioneer family as they found rest for the night along the banks of Camp Creek where today's Camp Creek and lower down, Tollgate campgrounds are located today.

For many years, the Department of Fish and Wildlife stocked Camp Creek with rainbows, but today ODFW manages the fishery for its resident coastal cutthroat.

Camp Creek is managed for the benefit of native cutthroat. The lower reaches of the stream offer the best access and fishing. Photo by Gary Lewis

The creek can be seen on the south side of the highway in the vicinity of the Mirror Lake trailhead and parallels the road for almost seven miles on its way to its confluence with the Zigzag River. Fishing is restricted to artificial fly or lure. No bait is allowed.

Much of the creek is steep and fast and the fish have to work hard in the swift current. A lot of the energy that would be used in growing is burnt off in just staying alive. Five-inchers are common and a ten-incher is a trophy, but the fishing can be fast, especially away from the trail.

The lower reaches of the creek offer the best access and the best angling. As the creek gathers water there are more trout per mile. Areas of slower water will yield the biggest fish. Here it's a good idea to match the hatch with dry flies. Roll casts and dapping will bring more fish to hand than pick-up-and-lay-down casting.

When there are no bugs in evidence above the surface, check spider webs for clues and pick up rocks to check the bug life. Try to match the size and shape of nymphs with tungsten-beaded bugs. Because most of the fish are small, crimp the barbs on your hooks before you fish and turn the trout loose fast to give them the best chance at survival.

Both Tollgate and Camp Creek campgrounds offer a feeling of seclusion amid the towering cedars and firs. Well developed sites include fire pits and leveled tent sites. Late at night, take a moment and listen to the water and the crackle of the fire and to the wind in the tops of the trees. You are hearing it the way the pioneers heard it on the old Barlow Road on the last leg of a long journey to the valley of the Willamette.

Directions

Take Highway 26 east from Sandy, pass through Zigzag and Rhododendron and look for Camp Creek on the south side of the highway. Tollgate and Camp Creek are the best landmarks.

Foxgloves provide a splash of color in spring and early summer.
Photo by Gary Lewis

Resources

Nearest cities/towns:
Rhododendron, Zigzag, Government Camp

Accommodations:
Mount Hood Village

Camping:
Tollgate, Camp Creek

Tackle:
The Fly Fishing Shop, Welches
www.flyfishusa.com

Visitor information:
Mt. Hood Area Chamber
www.mthood.org
503-622-3017

Still Creek

Length	12+ miles
Regulations	Artificial fly & lure Catch & Release
Difficulty	Moderate
Elevation at source	3,800 feet
Elevation at mouth	1,600 feet

Species: Cutthroat, rainbow trout

Best Methods: Fly fishing

Tips: Fish beadhead nymphs or wet flies in tandem

It was the summer I was 18 when my friend Ryan showed me a little stream called Still Creek on the western slope of Mount Hood.

My uncle Jon had built for me an ultralight trout spinning rod and, armed with a boxful of black Rooster Tails, we hunted rainbow trout in the log-jammed pools dappled with the sun that winked through the alders.

Even then we marveled at the big cedars that cast their shadows over the stream.

I wondered from whence came the name. No part of Still Creek that I was familiar with was still. Perhaps someone had a still way up one of the tributaries way back when.

We had to bypass a lot of riffles to find water deep enough to run our spinners, but the fish rewarded our efforts. These were hatchery rainbows that averaged 10 to 12 inches. My biggest went 15 inches and fought like a steelhead, burning line off the reel, running and jumping. Never in those years did I catch a cutthroat, but I watched Ryan do it once.

He spotted a little riffle up against a brushy bank and he worked it, patient, cast after cast. I thought he wasted his time until I saw his rod bend with the weight of a good fish. When he brought it to hand, he shouted across the creek.

"It's a native cutthroat." It looked to be about 11 inches. He turned it loose and we avoided fishing that spot again in the future. It was the next year when we heard that Still Creek would no longer be planted with hatchery trout, in order to restore the native cutthroat fishery and protect wild salmon and steelhead habitat. It was hard not to agree with the decision.

On a July day, I returned to Still Creek and found it, unlike many of the favorite places of my youth, little changed.

In fact, one of the trees I used to cross the creek is still there. I climbed up the same path through the root wad that I had scampered when I was a teenager.

With a drop of 2,200 feet in just over 12 miles, Still Creek's character is sub-alpine with riffle after riffle broken by large boulders and short pools. Photo by Robert Parrish

The only difference was that no bark was left on the fallen monarch.

Instead of a spinning rod, this time I was armed with a 10-foot, 4-weight fly rod, better suited to a creek with so much pocket water.

The small marabou muddler hit the water and a trout streaked up through the riffle and smacked it. About seven inches, I judged. On the next cast, a bigger fish flashed at the surface, grabbed the fly and showed me its flank. Just like a cutthroat. But in another moment he spit the hook.

With a smile on my face, I worked upstream and rested the good water. Twenty minutes later, I returned to the log jam with a No. 14 beadhead Caddis Pupa and a No. 20 Olive Sparkle whatzit. On the first drift, the line tightened and I brought a fingerling up for inspection. This one was no rainbow or cutthroat, but a baby coho unless I missed my guess.

When again the leader straightened out and the rod bent, it was an eight-inch cutthroat, heavily spotted on back and sides; brilliant crimson slashes beneath its jaws, the tips of its fins orange and tipped in white.

With the hook removed, the fish kicked away and vanished into a tangle of timber.

Still Creek gets its start near the 3,800-foot mark on the south slope of Mount Hood near Trillium Lake, Ski Bowl and Multorpor. The same slopes that skiers traverse all winter channel the snowmelt into the creek bed. For a few miles, the creek bears south and west then swings back north and west to parallel Camp Creek to the confluence at the Zigzag River.

With a drop of 2,200 feet in just over 12 miles, the creek's character is alpine to sub-alpine with riffle after riffle broken by large boulders and short pools, often at log jams. The water is clear and clean without a lot of food and the trout are vulnerable to bushy dry flies, as well as small streamers and beadhead nymphs. In the short runs, the fish have to make a quick decision about what is edible and what is not. Attractor flies can turn a lot of fish.

At one wide spot in the road, we found two Caterpillars and a sign from The Freshwater Trust that announced a side channel restoration in progress. We found cables that tied log jams together and woven wire to prevent erosion of the bank at critical points. Expected benefits of the project include refuge for juvenile fish, more spawning gravel, more fish prey (insects) and a reduction in damage to fish habitat by flooding.

I suspected that, if I was patient enough, I could find an 11-inch cutthroat that would take a fly, perhaps a pair of them.

It is nice to find a creek that is better now than the way I remembered it.

The Still Creek Road follows the stream for much of its length, offering glimpses of water through stands of firs and old-growth cedar. Alders line the banks and downed timber offers pathways to the angler that doesn't want to get his or her feet wet.

Here the rocks are slick with moss, water and slime. Wading boots with felt might offer the best grip.

A classic west-slope mountain creek, access trails begin at parking places at fizzle out where logs cross the water. Angler trails lead up one side or the other, but most fishermen stay near the waterline.

When we fished it, the trout averaged 7 to 10 inches and did not seem to care whether our imitations were suggestive of caddis, mayfly, stonefly or sculpin.

Steelhead may be found in the creek in the summer months and coho salmon may be present in September and October.

Still Creek is managed for fishing with artificial fly and lure only, catch and release for trout. Fishing for salmon and steelhead is closed.

Directions

From Highway 26, take the Still Creek Road south for 3/10 of a mile then bear right on Forest Road 12. A paved road charts the course of the creek through a community of summer homes. Public access begins where the pavement ends at almost three miles from the highway.

To reach the headwaters from Highway 26, look for the sign to Still Creek Campground, located east of the Highway 26 summit near Trillium Lake.

Resources

Nearest cities/towns:
Rhododendron, Zigzag, Government Camp

Accommodations:
Mount Hood Village

Camping:
Primitive

Tackle:
The Fly Fishing Shop, Welches
www.flyfishusa.com

Visitor information:
Mt. Hood Area Chamber
www.mthood.org
503-622-3017

Confluence Fly Shop • Follow on Facebook

Gorge Creeks

Regulations .... Artificial fly & lure
                                    Catch & Release

Difficulty .... Moderate

Species .... Cutthroat, rainbow trout

Best Methods: Fly fishing

Tips: Fish beadhead nymphs or wet flies in tandem

The Columbia River Gorge is a magnificent Canyon that stretches for over 80 miles as the big river cuts a path through the Cascade Mountains to the Pacific Ocean. Due to its incredibly scenic nature and importance to tourism and recreation, the Gorge was deemed a National Scenic Area in 1986 and as such receives some protection from industry and development.

Though the Gorge began to form millions of years ago during the Miocene Period, the most significant changes to the landscape occurred near the end of the last ice age when the Missoula Floods repeatedly raced down the Gorge and carved the steep, dramatic landscape that we have today. These floods were the result of the constant rupturing of the ice dam that formed glacial Lake Missoula. When the ice dam burst, it would send a destructive torrent of ice, water and debris that would inundate much of Eastern Washington and the Willamette Valley.

Imagine a flood having an estimated flow of ten times that of ALL the world's rivers combined, and you begin to get a picture of the scale of it all. It is estimated that at least a few of these floods reached as high as Crown Point in the Gorge, and the water raged at speeds of over 60 miles per hour! With forces of nature like this at work, dramatic geological changes took place literally overnight, leaving us with the incredibly scenic landscape we see today.

The beauty of the Columbia River Gorge beckons outdoorswomen and men to a wide variety of activities in its stunning surroundings. Hikers enjoy the many trails leading to a multitude of beautiful waterfalls. Windsurfing, kite-boarding and rock climbing lure the adventurous. Water skiing, boating and sailing are popular on the Columbia River. Camping, biking, photography, bird watching… the list goes on. Visitors go to Bonneville Dam to view salmon and sturgeon. Day trippers from the Portland/Vancouver area head to Cascade Locks to buy salmon and soak up the sights, then head up the Gorge to the hip town of Hood River, where excellent food and beverage await, including one of the crown jewels of Oregon, the Full Sail Brewery. Hood River is also world renowned for the excellent produce it grows. On top of all of this going on in the Gorge, add sport fishing.

The view from Vista House at Crown Point looks up the Columbia River Gorge deep into salmon, trout and steelhead country. Photo by Robert Campbell

Obviously the big draw in the Gorge is the Columbia River itself, with over two million Chinook, coho, sockeye and steelhead running upstream on a good year. While most of the smaller tributaries on the Oregon side are closed to salmon fishing in season, there are still plentiful opportunities to catch salmon and steelhead from the larger streams like the Sandy, Hood and Deschutes Rivers. What the smaller tributaries do offer, however, are "bubble" fisheries at their mouths for salmon and steelhead, as well as catch-and-release trout fishing for wild trout in an incredible setting.

Approximately 10 miles east of Troutdale is tiny Bridal Veil Creek. Bridal Veil offers some of the most beautiful little cutthroat trout you will find anywhere. They are somewhat reminiscent of those caught from the Oak Grove Fork of the Clackamas River, being very heavily spotted and having bright orange fins. The best fishing on the creek is above the falls and is reached via Palmer Mill Road, a steep, dangerous, mostly single lane road with few pull-outs. Drive slowly. After about a three-mile ascent, you will reach the creek and can bushwhack your way up or down this plunge pool fishery. This is extremely rugged terrain and should only be attempted by fit anglers. Tucked into a beautiful little canyon, the creek is well-shaded and remains cool even in the heat of summer, which makes it a great option on a searing July day. Take your camera.

Many of the other smaller creeks in the Gorge have wild trout populations as well, including Multnomah, Oneonta, McCord, and more. Larger streams like Eagle Creek, Tanner Creek and Herman Creek have runs of salmon and steelhead, though you will want to check the regulations for each creek to determine open seasons.

The lure of many Gorge creeks, however, are the large numbers of summer steelhead, coho and Chinook that they attract during the summer and fall migrations. One negative side effect of all those dams on the Columbia is that the water in the reservoirs behind them is heated by the summer sun and becomes much warmer than it would be if the river were free-flowing. It is not uncommon for summer flows on the lower Columbia to reach 70 degrees or more, which is toward the upper end of tolerance for salmon and steelhead.

Above all else, salmon and steelhead need clean, cold water to survive. Several of the Gorge creeks emit enough flow into the Columbia to produce a cold water "bubble" that attracts the salmon and steelhead into a more comfortable, healthy environment. Often the fish will keg up in these areas in huge numbers to rest before heading upstream.

One such location is just upstream of Bonneville Dam at the mouth of Eagle Creek. Eagle Creek is home to Cascade Hatchery, an ODFW managed facility authorized by the Mitchell Act that began operating in 1959 to enhance declining wild runs of salmon on the Columbia. The hatchery raises coho salmon which return to the creek in plentiful numbers each fall. The creek also offers a cool water refuge to

Resources

Nearest cities/towns:
Troutdale, Cascade Locks, Hood River, The Dalles

Tackle:
The Fly Fishing Shop, Welches
Gorge Fly Shop
Fly Fishing Strategies
Gorge Outfitters

Fisherman's Marine and Outdoor
Delta Park
503 283-0044

Visitor information:
Hood River County
Chamber of Commerce
www.hoodriver.org

The Dalles Chamber of Commerce
www.thedalleschamber.com
541-296-2231

A school of coho stages in Eagle Creek waiting for rain to prompt their migration. Photo by Robert Campbell

There are some nice trout in Eagle Creek, but they aren't easy in the gin-clear water. Photo by Robert Campbell

Chinook, coho and steelhead that have just conquered Bonneville's fish ladders. The numbers of fish that amass off the mouth of Eagle Creek in September and October can be staggering.

Small boats can launch on a gravel bar below the mainline railroad bridge and row or motor a short distance out to fish the Columbia. Larger boats can put in at Cascade Locks and motor down to this fishery. The creek flows across a shallow basalt shelf before dropping off into 30-plus feet of water. This unique situation lets anglers anchor their craft in a few feet of water while fishing gear in deep water only a few feet away. The area immediately in front of Eagle Creek is popular with bobber and egg fishermen, while further out a productive troll fishery has developed where anglers use lead, flasher and herring to troll for the river's salmon.

Eagle Creek is also very popular with hikers headed up to its many scenic waterfalls, though the trail has some dangerous cliffs so it's probably not the best place for small children and pets. The creek also harbors both cutthroat and rainbow trout for catch-and-release angling, yet they are notoriously difficult to catch when the creek runs crystal-clear during the summer months. Use stealth tactics to get in range of the fish, for they will bolt into hiding if they see you. A No. 14 Elk Hair Caddis is all you will need to catch trout here, that is, if they don't see you coming. Be prepared to nymph subsurface if the trout don't rise to dries. Small spinners and spoons will take decent trout from pockets and plunge pools around boulders. There are some surprisingly nice trout in Eagle Creek, though they are not easy. At summer flows it is relatively easy for fit, experienced anglers to wade the creek upstream of the trailhead parking lot, though felt or studded soles are recommended on the extremely slick boulders.

Eagle Creek is closed to salmon and steelhead for most of the season from the mainline railroad bridge upstream, affording the fish sanctuary to do their thing. The gin-clear water of Eagle Creek makes it an excellent place to view salmon in a small stream environment. There are many places between the hatchery and trailhead parking lot to conveniently view fish in the creek along the access road. Children delight in getting up close and personal with such majestic creatures.

Further upstream near the town of Cascade Locks, Herman Creek flows into a lagoon where its cooler water draws salmon and steelhead in off the mainstem. Oxbow Hatchery is located on Herman Creek and is used for egg incubation and early rearing of coho, spring Chinook and sockeye. No adult salmon are collected at the hatchery for spawning, and there are none released into the creek, so all of the Chinook and coho that you see spawning in Herman Creek in October and early November are wild fish or strays from another hatchery.

The fishery at the Herman Creek Lagoon really gets going around Labor Day as the Columbia heats up to the point that the fish start looking for relief in cooler water. The number of summer steelhead that sometimes flood into the lagoon can be phenomenal, and when they are on the snap this is one of the most frenetic steelhead fisheries you will see anywhere. Anglers use a variety of bait, including prawns, eggs and coon shrimp to catch steelhead here. This is not the best place to cast lures as the sheer numbers of fish in tight quarters make it difficult to use hardware without snagging fish.

For decades the lagoon and its channel that lead out to the Columbia have also been a popular fly fishing area for steelhead, with small brown, purple, orange or black Comet-style flies quite popular. This pattern has come to be known locally as "The Herman Creek Special," and is available at the fly shop in Fisherman's Marine and Outdoor. A No. 6 or No. 8 is standard. Cast this fly out on a clear intermediate line or short sink-tip, and vary the retrieve and depth until you find out what the fish are responding to on any given day. This area can get quite crowded with anglers so it is important to be able to control your fish. Use an appropriate leader of ten-pound test minimum, and nothing lighter than an eight-weight rod.

Later in the fall when the salmon begin to show up, the steelhead scatter and head upriver. While the coho and Chinook can be somewhat more difficult to entice to strike, they can be made to bite by the patient bait or fly angler. By late September the lower reaches of the creek itself have filled up with spawning salmon, and like Eagle Creek, Herman Creek is a great place to bring the kids to watch these amazing creatures complete their mission.

Whether you come to the Columbia River Gorge to hike, camp, fish or sightsee, the gorge is a truly unique area. The scenery is beautiful. Wildlife abounds. The towns of The Dalles, Hood River and Cascade Locks are filled with friendly people who define the Pacific Northwest Lifestyle: hard working, hard playing, with a deep love of family, friends, the land and water. A favorite pastime of mine is to take somebody from out of town up to Crown Point and have them look east up the Gorge on a clear day. The reaction is always the same, and it's the kind of moment that makes you proud to be an Oregonian.

Upper Bridal Veil Creek offers beautiful wild cutthroat in a gorgeous, challenging setting. Photo by Robert Campbell

Big Leaf Maple paint the landscape during Autumn in the Columbia River Gorge. Photo by Robert Campbell

Protected from anglers, a mixed school of coho and chinook fill a pool on Eagle Creek, a great place to take kids to watch salmon up close. Photo by Robert Campbell

Harriett Lake

Size ....23 acres

Depth.....................................Deepest at dam

Trail ....On road side of lake, following up
             and downstream along the river

Difficulty .... Wheelchair Accessible

Elevation .... 2,037 feet

GPS Coordinates: .... N 45 04.420
                                          W 121 57.567

Species: Rainbow, cutthroat, brown, and
brook trout

Best Methods: Fly, still-fishing

Tips: Bring a float tube.

You can fish Harriet Lake, a 23-acre reservoir on the Oak Grove Fork of the Clackamas, without a raft, a canoe or a float tube, but a boat provides a decided advantage. Harriett is well-known for trophy browns, rainbows, cutthroats and brook trout. The upper end of the lake is best for the biggest fish, especially early and late in the day. Two boat launches make access easy and bank anglers set up along the upper north shore.

When we showed up on a sunny summer Saturday afternoon, we found that Harriet had been "discovered" by bait fishermen. The interesting thing to note was that there were no boats on the water. And, to my way of thinking, the best water was only reachable by a float tube, pontoon boat or a fishing kayak.

We launched our boats and tubes and spread out just beyond the casting range of the bank anglers. I tied on a rubber-legged beadhead Hare's Ear with a Callibaetis Nymph on the dropper. In two hours, I brought nine trout to hand - two browns and seven rainbows. The biggest was 13 inches. At first all the

*A nice brown taken at Harriett Lake
Photo by Steve Nehl*

The Oak Grove Fork of the Clackamas feeds into Harriett Lake. Photo by Gary Lewis

takes were below the surface. When a few mayflies began to hatch, I switched to a soft hackle mayfly emerger pattern and watched the fish swirl when they took it.

The Department of Fish and Wildlife stocks Harriet in April, May, June, July and August, which means that good fishing can be had throughout the season.

Anglers that work this lake from the bank prefer worms fished on a sliding sinker rig. Some use jar baits or salmon eggs to good effect. Try Rooster Tail spinners early and late in the day.

It seems that fly fishermen do as well or better on this lake than the bait anglers. But the best fly fishing is from a pontoon boat or a float tube. The flooded timber makes this lake food-rich with plenty of structure and character. The head of the lake has a riffle, pools and islands like a river. Trout feed all day in the three- to five-foot water around the stumps and floating logs. Oxygenated water and shadows concentrate the fish. If the wind blows a riffle on the water, the trout will take dry flies.

Hatches of mayflies, midges, caddis, stonefly, damsels and dragonflies may occur throughout the season. Carry several sizes and colors of ant patterns. At certain times of the spring and summer, flying ants will hit the water.

Directions

Take Hwy 224 from Estacada into Mt. Hood National Forest. About a mile past Ripplebrook Ranger Station, follow Forest Rd. 57 toward Timothy Lake. After about 6 miles Rd. 57 crosses Oak Grove Fork. Take Forest Rd. 4630 west one mile to Harriet Lake.

Gold Bead Shaggy Hare's Ear
Tied by Pete Ouelette

Ever since the day I first picked up a fly rod, the Hare's Ear, in all its variants, has been a favorite. It is still in my go-to trout box in the spring, when Callibaetis are hatching. In May and June, a gold bead soft-hackle Hare's Ear, dead-drifted, is deadly in the pocket water.

The unkempt look of the Gold Bead Shaggy Hare's Ear makes this favorite even more appealing with its ability to suggest a variety of trout foods. Just vary the retrieve and figure out how the fish want to eat it.

Tie this one with brown thread on a No. 10-12 Tiemco 3761. Slide a gold bead up to the eye and tie a tail of Hungarian partridge fibers. For the body, use hare's mask fur and leave the guard hairs in. Rib with gold oval wire. Wrap a sparse partridge hackle and finish with a collar of dubbing behind the bead.

High Rocks Wilderness

Number of Lakes 16

Size Range .... 2 to 20 acres, with 8 lakes .... larger than 9 acres

Trails .... 1 to 5 miles, easy to moderate elevation gains

Difficulty .... Steep climb, good trail

Elevation .... 3,650 to 5,000 feet Most are in the 4,000 foot range

Species: Stocked brook trout, rainbow trout and cutthroat trout

Best Methods: Water-filled casting bubble for casting distance and your favorite small spinner, fly or chunk of nitecrawler. Plunking power bait is also effective.

Lakes in the High Rocks Wilderness are characterized by clean, clear water and timbered slopes that go right to the waterline. A float tube or a raft can give the angler an advantage. Photo by Dave Kilhefner

The High Rock Wilderness Lakes hold many good memories for me. I've been fishing them since I started driving in 1980 and the beautiful scenery and dependable fishing keeps me coming back year after year.

Situated in the heavily forested western slopes of the Cascade Foothills, these lakes have many common features; a rock slide along one side, a tiny outlet creek at the other and brushy shorelines that often make spin casting difficult and fly casting nearly impossible.

During low snow years you can access these lakes from May thru the end of October, but the most popular months are July, August and September.

You'll need a Northwest Forest Pass to park at most trailheads.

Once at the lake of your choice, if you want to catch a limit of trout, by far the easiest way to do it is with an ultra-light spin rod with 4-pound line, a small water filled casting bubble for casting distance, a three foot long leader and a small 1-inch chunk of nitecrawler for bait. These lakes all have a shoreline shelf that feed fish cruise. Find a rock or log to stand on, ignore the fish rising in the middle of the lake and look for fish cruising or rising along the shelf line then start casting. Let your offering sink a few feet below the surface and slowly retrieve; there's no need to let it sink deeper than four to five feet because all you'll do is hang up on the shelf line or submerged logs.

When packing into a high lake in warm weather, keep your nitecrawlers alive by wrapping the bait container in a wet bandana. The evaporation will provide enough cooling to keep your bait alive. Since I use small chunks of bait, I've never gone thru more

than a few nitecrawlers in a weekend trip so a dozen is more than enough.

The best bite period is usually from mid-day to early afternoon when the water temperature warms and insect activity is at its peak and there is almost always a Callibaetis mayfly hatch during this time. Ants falling from overhanging trees also attract feeding trout.

Brook trout tend to be streaky biters so you need to be fishing when they are biting, which is usually a couple hours in the early afternoon. Rainbow and Cutthroat trout, which the ODFW has been stocking more and more lately, are all day feeders but definitely turn on in the early afternoon too.

Most trout are in the 6 to 10 inch size range but holdovers can run to 18 inches.

Given the brush, determined fly anglers often pack in small rafts or float tubes. The most popular lakes for this are Shellrock Lake (1 mile hike), Middle Rock Lake (1.5 miles) and even Serene Lake (3 miles). You can drive to Hideaway Lake but given the easy access, the fish are more educated. The rest of the lakes are either too small & shallow or too far (Shining Lake-4.5 miles) to make packing in a float tube worthwhile.

I'm a fairly serious fly angler. Good fly fishing is available but you'll need to be able to roll cast well to deal with the brushy shoreline or pack in a float tube. Both of these things increase the time and effort required and when I fly fish, I tend to disappear for hours on end. Given this, if I'm on a family or group trip I stick to spin fishing so I can quickly catch a few trout and enjoy quality family time in this beautiful natural area.

During the summer months, the water often gets warm enough for swimming. It's a very refreshing way to cool off after a summer hike. If you plan on swimming bring a pair of water socks or something to protect your feet. The rocks on the bottom of the lakes are sharp and slippery.

The High Rock lakes are a great place to take someone on their first backpacking trip during the months of August and September when the weather is usually good and the bugs are down. My personal favorite "lake tour" is to start at the Shellrock Lake Trailhead and hike make the 5-mile hike to Serene Lake. This takes you by Shellrock Lake, the Rock Lakes and if your legs are still springy, you can go all the way to Serene, camp overnight and hike out the next day.

The lakes have populations of crawfish, which are fun to catch and good to eat too. I discovered this at Serene Lake on day while the crawdads feasted on my string of fish sitting in the lake. Since that day I gut the fish immediately after catching them and let them cool in lakeside shade. My kids like to use the guts tied on a string to catch crawdads. If the crawdads are sizeable, we keep them to eat with dinner. Cooked in boiling water, the tails and sometimes even the claws make a nice appetizer for the evening meal.

Resources

Nearest cities/towns:
Estacada

Camping:
Clackamas River Ranger District
Mt. Hood National Forest
503-630-6861

Tackle:
Estacada Tackle
503-630-7424

Great American Tackle Shop
503-650-2662

Visitor information:
Estacada Chamber of Commerce
www.estacadachamber.org
503-630-3483

For the best trout fishing action, plan backpacking trips for August and September. Photo by Dave Kilhefner

Mirror Lake

Size	8 acres
Depth	8 feet
Trail	1.4 miles
Difficulty	Steep climb, good trail

Elevation:

Trailhead	3,350 feet
Lake	4,108 feet

Species: Rainbow, cutthroat trout

Best Methods: Fly and casting bubble

Tips: Fish crayfish patterns or crayfish plugs

High in the Sandy River watershed, Mirror Lake is a small jewel that, on a clear day, reflects a perfect image of the mountain. The trailhead to Mirror Lake is not hard to find, look for it on the south side of the highway about two miles west of Government Camp.

The difficult thing about fishing Mirror Lake is the timing. Most hikes start early in the morning. The trail winds uphill around the back side of Tom, Dick and Harry Mountain and deposits the hiker on the lakeshore, winded from the climb. Most hikers start on the way back down well before dark, leaving the lake unfished during the peak periods of fishing. The way to fish both morning and evening is to camp in one of the primitive sites above the lake. Bring the mosquito repellent.

Mirror Lake is eight acres in size and reaches a depth of about eight feet or so. Fallen timber provides good habitat for rainbow trout and cutthroats. When we fished it, on a late July morning, we caught cutthroat to about eight inches, likely stocked as fingerlings the summer before. We found good numbers of crayfish in the muddy shallows, which speaks to the possible food source for the biggest trout in the lake.

A nice, well-marked trail leads to this iconic Mount Hood lake. From some angles, long casts are necessary to reach the deeper water. Photo by Gary Lewis

Best fishing will be in June when the trail opens and again late in the season after the kids go back to school.

Expect the trout to run six to ten inches, but bigger ones are there. A float tube could be packed in up the trail, but it isn't necessary. Anglers equipped with spinning rods and fly and bubble rigs will do the best. For bigger trout, use crayfish imitations.

Directions

On Highway 26, drive east toward Government Camp. Look for a large parking area and the trailhead about two miles west of Government Camp and one mile west of Multorpor on the south side of the highway.

Crawdads are a major protein source for Mirror Lake rainbows and cutthroat. Photo by Gary Lewis

Resources

Nearest cities/towns:
Government Camp

Accommodations:
Government Camp resorts

Camping:
Trillium Lake Campground
Camp Creek Campground

Tackle:
The Fly Fishing Shop - Welches
Top Stop Food & Fuel

Visitor information:
Mt. Hood Area Chamber
www.mthood.org
503-622-3017

Bill Brackett starts up the 1.4-mile trail to Mirror Lake. Photo by Gary Lewis

North Fork Reservoir

Size	325 acres
Depth	120 feet
Trail	1.4 miles
Difficulty	Easy/moderate
Elevation	665 feet

Species: Rainbow, cutthroat, bull, brook , brown trout

Best Methods: Trolling, bank angling

Tips: Trolling is productive and a slow troll pays off with more trout.

Within easy driving distance of Portland, just six miles east of Estacada, North Fork Reservoir is a popular destination for both bank anglers and boaters.

There is some native fish production, but the angling effort is concentrated on hatchery fish. The Department of Fish and Wildlife stocks close to 80,000 legal rainbows from May through September. Hatchery trout average 10 to 12 inches. Only adipose fin-clipped trout may be retained. Wild rainbows, cutthroat, brook trout, brown trout and bull trout must be released.

Construction of the 207-foot-high dam at the confluence of the North Fork and the mainstem Clackamas was finished in 1958 and the water began to stack up behind the dam. A great fishery was born. This narrow, deep, electrical power generation pool stretches four miles into the western slope of the Cascades.

The topography of the lake bottom is rugged, with older volcanic flows carved by inlet streams. Above the surface, the ground rises steep with its slopes densely forested with Douglas firs. Much of the lakeshore is private but undeveloped.

The trout are easily taken on trolling gear. Dick

The Oregon Department of Fish and Wildlife stocks 80,000 legal rainbows throughout the spring and summer. For good action without a lot of competition, try this pretty reservoir in September and early October.
Photo by Gary Lewis

Nite spoons tipped with bait are deadly. Rainbows here also like to grab small crankbaits. If trout are found in large schools, rig with a clear plastic float and cast a pink plastic worm on a red No. 6 bait hook. Crank it back very slow, pausing to let the bait flutter down through the fish.

Some of the best angling is found in the faster water at the upper end of the lake, near the marina and at the boat launches. Popular trolling areas include the log boom in front of the dam, the north shore, near the lower launch and under the power lines.

Thanks to snow melt high in the Cascades, the water is cold in the early season. Fishing action picks up in May and continues into October. For the angler without a boat, good bank fishing can be found at the wheelchair-accessible ramp, at the log booms, near the North Fork inlet and close to the boat launches. These are good areas for the angler with a float tube or a canoe to explore in calm water before the ski boats begin to take over at midday.

Most services are available in nearby Estacada. Groceries, fishing tackle, and boat and motor rentals are available at the concession store located at Promontory Park. A boat dock and launching area are next to the store. The store at Promontory Park opens in mid-May and closes mid-September.

For people with disabilities, the park has an accessible restroom, campsites, boat dock and rentable patio boats.

Anglers note: there is no speed limit on the lower half of the reservoir, but the upper half has a 10-mph limit.

Directions

Nearby, Small Fry Lake (within Promontory Park) is a great place to take the kids (age 17 and under) for a chance at a 'keeper.' The lake is one acre in size and is a great place to teach the kids to fish.

Resources

Nearest cities/towns:
Estacada

Accommodations:
Red Fox Motel 503-630-4243

Camping:
Promontory Park

Tackle:
Fisherman's Marine & Outdoor
503-630-7424

Estacada Tackle
503-630-7424

Great American Tackle Shop
503-650-2662

Visitor information:
Estacada Chamber of Commerce
www.estacadachamber.org
503-630-3483

Don Lewis teased up this nice hatchery trout with a slow-trolled Dick Nite spoon.

Try still-fishing or wind-drifting for rainbows off the point at Promontory Park. Photo by Gary Lewis

Small Fry Lake

Size .... 1 acre

Depth .... 8 feet

Regulations .... Limited to youth anglers 17 years old or younger, limit two trout

Elevation .... 665 feet

Species: Stocked rainbow trout

Best Methods: Bait or lure

Tips: For catch and release fishing, use a fly and bubble presentation

If you have young children that you would like to introduce to trout fishing at an easy venue, then Small Fry Lake is for you! This pond is located 7 miles east of Estacada on Highway 224 in Promontory Park, a PGE managed recreational facility on North Fork Reservoir.

After leaving the highway, the route to the lake is signed well enough that even a distracted parent driving a mini-van full of yahoos should have no problem finding it. Gratefully, there is a restroom conveniently located near the parking lot. Corral your monkeys and enjoy the short walk down the hill to the lake.

Located in a small depression hemmed in between the park access road and North Fork Reservoir, Small Fry is a relatively controlled environment where children can have an easy introduction to trout fishing. You will, however, still need to keep an eye on the goonies because the shoreline does drop-off abruptly into deep water, and there are some trails nearby that lead to steep terrain.

The Oregon Department of Fish and Wildlife maintains a routine stocking schedule at Small Fry, so there are usually plenty of trout on hand to command

Don't let its size fool you, Small Fry is usually packed with trout!. Photo by Robert Campbell

With her custom pink Lamiglas rod this young angler fishes in style!
Photo by Robert Campbell

the attention of young anglers. The fishing is straight forward: either use Power Bait fished up from the bottom, or, a night crawler fished under a bobber. Small spinners and spoons will also arouse some interest from the fish, especially early in the season when the water is cold. It doesn't take many groups to make it crowded here, so parents should maintain constant supervision over their anglers to make sure that the only thing being pierced by sharp hooks are the fish.

The trout are of the standard 9-11 inch cookie cutter variety, but every now and then a surprise hold-over is caught which generally causes a stir among the Little Rascal Angling Fraternity. We once saw a young boy parade around the lake with his 12-inch prize on a stringer, head held high, as though he had caught a 30-pound spring chinook. And all kidding aside, that's kind of the point of Small Fry Lake, to get your kids out in the fresh

air looking at trees and bugs and trout instead of a TV or computer screen. And, to hopefully spark an interest in our natural world as well as a lifelong love of all things wild.

If your troop soon tires of fishing, there are plenty of other activity options nearby, including hiking trails, picnic areas, or boating or swimming on North Fork Reservoir. Normally there are supplies available at Promontory Park Store and Marina, but these facilities are currently closed until 2016 for the construction of fish passage improvements. No worries, gas, food and other supplies are just down the road in the town of Estacada.

North Fork Reservoir is also heavily stocked with trout throughout the season and is another option for young anglers. Trout from North Fork must have a clipped adipose fin, which means they are of hatchery origin and not a young wild steelhead or salmon.

Resources

Nearest cities/towns:
Estacada

Accommodations:
Red Fox Motel 503-630-4243

Camping:
Promontory Park

Tackle:
Fisherman's Marine & Outdoor
503-630-7424

Estacada Tackle
503-630-7424

Visitor information:
Estacada Chamber of Commerce
www.estacadachamber.org
503-630-3483

That didn't take very long! Now, back to playing with ants.
Photo by Robert Campbell

Timothy Lake

Size .... 1,300 acres at full pool

Maximum Depth ....80 feet (full pool)

Elevation .... 3217 feet

Species: Wild and stocked rainbow, wild cutthroat, brook trout, kokanee salmon

Best Methods: Trolling, casting lures, bait fishing—it all works here—though fly fishers mimicking natural forage will catch the most and biggest trout.

Tips: Fish near to the shoreline around stumps and weed beds where food production is the greatest.

Timothy Lake is a reservoir created in 1956 when Portland General Electric dammed the Oak Grove Fork of the Clackamas River for hydroelectric production. The resulting lake became the largest body of water in the Mt. Hood National Forest, as well as one of the most popular for recreation. Timothy has a broad, circular shape, which is contrary to most mountain reservoirs, and gives the lake a natural feel and appearance.

With seven beautiful campgrounds on the lake, several species of trout to fish for, and a nice 13-mile trail encircling it all, it's easy to see why Timothy Lake is such a draw. Add to that its proximity to Portland, easy access and 10 mile-per-hour speed limit that keeps the MTV beach party scene to a minimum, it is clear why Timothy is such a popular family destination.

Timothy Lake also happens to have good—sometimes excellent—fishing for a variety of trout and kokanee in a wonderful mountain setting. I have probably spent more time trout fishing on Timothy Lake than any other still water, and I can say without a doubt that Timothy is the most underrated trout water in the state.

Far too many anglers dismiss Timothy Lake as nothing more than a classic put-and-take fishery designed to appease the angling hordes, when really it is much more than that. Yes, ODFW continues to dump thousands of hatchery "catchables" each season into the lake, but there is more going on here for the angler who truly gets to know Timothy. For instance, there are wild rainbows here that go well beyond the magical 20-inch mark, and trophy brook trout that can be measured in pounds. And while the native cutthroat in Timothy don't get quite as large as the brookies and rainbows, they are wild mountain trout that are amongst the most beautiful fish you will ever behold.

I've met many Timothy regulars who scoffed when told about the trophy trout fishing, with comments like, "I've been fishing Timothy for over 20 years and never caught a rainbow over 14 inches." So why does the angling potential of Timothy go unnoticed by so many anglers? Well, for starters, you just won't catch many large, cagey wild trout trolling wedding ring spinners behind a flasher out in the middle of the lake over barren water. Above all else, trout need cool, well-oxygenated water, ample food and good cover in the form of rocks, wood or weed beds. These are not attributes that you will find in 50-60 feet of water.

Probably more so than any other lake I have ever fished, it is absolutely imperative to focus your angling attention at Timothy to the littoral zones of the lake, that is, near the shorelines. Here in the shallows, food production is at its greatest, as penetrating sunlight supports weed and phytoplankton growth that in turn provides the food base for a variety of aquatic insects including midges, caddis, dragonflies, damselflies, mayflies and more. This forage base in turn attracts larger creatures like crawdads, small fry and immature amphibians. And all of the above attract the trout.

Timothy Lake is also sometimes called Timothy Meadows Reservoir, as this area was widely used by sheep herders who supplemented the native grasses with Timothy grass seed. These meadows were lined with intruding stands of timber that were cut before the basin was flooded by the dam, leaving behind plentiful "stump fields" that brook trout in particular

Exploring Timothy Lake by trail offers a unique view of this trout factory. Photo by Robert Campbell

There are some exceptional brook trout in Timothy if you know where to look.
Photo by Robert Campbell

Resources

Nearest cities/towns:
Government Camp

Camping:
Pine Point Campground
Hoodview Campground
Cove Campground
Gone Creek Campground
Meditation Point Campground
Oak Fork Campground
North Arm Campground
Clackamas Lake Campground
Timothy Lake Campground

Tackle:
Top Stop Food & Fuel

Visitor information:
Mt. Hood Area Chamber
www.mthood.org
503-622-3017

like to call home. Rock formations, boulder fields and scree slopes were also common in the area. Now under water, all of these features provide key habitat in the form of cover for the trout. Old creek channels flowing through otherwise shallow, undefined water also provide good cover for Timothy's larger trout. Locate areas like these along shoreline shallows where wave action entrains oxygen, add a weed bed or two, and you have found an area that will undoubtedly harbor some of the lake's larger specimens.

Never mind that such areas are typically only 5-15 feet deep, for this is where the trout will be. Far too many anglers seem to think that deep water equates to big fish, and that just isn't the case at Timothy and many other mountain lakes. In fact, if you fish too deep, often you will be fishing in water too cold and oxygen poor to support fish. Except during the heat of a particularly warm summer, your angling efforts should be focused on water of twenty feet deep or less. On the rare occasion I have taken trout at Timothy out of water 30-40 feet deep on the main body of the lake, but this was when surface temperatures were unusually high and the thermocline could be found much deeper than usual.

Another reason that anglers sometimes struggle to connect with Timothy's big trout is technique. As far as trout go, big wild fish are not as easily duped as tank raised fish that are used to being hand fed by humans.

The Grub Hub camp kitchen sets up in three minutes and holds a Camp Chef stove and all the utensils. Photo by Gary Lewis

Early in the season while the water is still cold, you can catch Timothy's larger trout on bait, though you will do better for larger fish on nightcrawlers or crawdad tails than you will on paste baits in my experience. Likewise, casting lures early in the season with little or no weight is a good technique for connecting with big rainbows and brook trout. But by far the best way to connect with Timothy's monster trout, especially the huge brook trout, is fly fishing.

Big trout are not stupid, and at Timothy they seem to know that a shiny bauble being ripped around the lake at 5 miles-per-hour behind a wildly erratic light show in the form of a flasher or lake troll is not natural feed. For the best success at Timothy or elsewhere when targeting trophy fish, you will by far have the most success if you learn what items comprise the trout's natural diet, and then do your best to mimic them. In most lake fishing this means aquatic insects, crawdads and leeches, and these items are best imitated by flies. I started fishing at Timothy Lake in my youth, catching my very first brook trout there in 1978. But I, like so many other anglers, had no idea what kind of killer trout were present until I later became adept at fly fishing.

In certain areas Timothy Lake has productive forage that the trout key in on. By mid-spring, the trout are attuned the natural rhythms and cycles and they schedule their days accordingly. Morning midge hatches are followed by mid-morning mayfly hatches which are followed by afternoon damselfly activity which is followed by evening crawdad and leech activity. The trout fall into somewhat reliable feeding patterns, and once the shrewd angler discerns what the trout's food is doing, he or she can get a pretty good idea what the trout are doing at any given moment as well. Don't stick with a #16 midge pupa fished under an indicator all day just because you caught three nice fish on it out of the gate; the trout may very well have moved on to another entrée.

I usually begin my angling day at Timothy by casting and retrieving a brown woolly bugger, crawdad or leech pattern. During the low light of early morning both crawdads and leeches are still active and big trout are on the prowl for them. If you go to Timothy specifically to target the brook trout that can reach five pounds or more, I would start by using a fly that mimics a crawdad 2-3 inches in length, for about half of all of the large brook trout that I have taken at Timothy had at least one of these in their stomachs. And I'm guessing that the other half were looking for one! If you catch a large brook trout at Timothy that you intend to release, gently feel its belly and

Find the trout food, find the trout. Shallow, weedy areas support the most aquatic insects. Photo by Robert Campbell

you will likely be able to detect the exoskeleton of a recently devoured crawdad. When it comes to brook trout, they are all delicious, but to me the best-tasting and most tender are the pan-sized 10-15 inchers. These are the ones that I harvest for a meal; the bigger fished are released to get even bigger and hopefully make more brook trout.

Mid-morning midge hatches at Timothy can be thick, and fishing a chironomid pupa under an indicator is deadly if you find the right color and size pattern to use, though this can be somewhat of a chess match as multiple species of midges may be hatching at once and the trout may be keyed on a particular type. Midge pupae in sizes 14-20 in black, grey and red are usually all that is needed.

Callibaetis mayflies are common at Timothy Lake in the shallow areas that have abundant weed growth. It is this bug that I mimic the most in my quest for large trout, for they are a prevalent forage that is widely available and particularly active on a daily basis. By far the majority of the trout I catch at Timothy during the day are on a #14 Callibaetis Nymph of some sort, though Mercer's Poxyback Cahill is my favorite.

Trails completely encircle Timothy, providing excellent access to the walk-in angler. Photo by Robert Campbell

Fish this nymph on a 10' long, 4X SeaGuar fluorocarbon leader with a painfully slow hand twist retrieve, and you will catch your fair share of nice trout at Timothy. And yes, I consider fluorocarbon tippet an absolute necessity when trout fishing in lakes if you want to have consistent results on larger fish. Having a leader that is nearly invisible is a decided advantage when targeting large, wary trout. SeaGuar is the best I have used.

Big brook trout have very sharp teeth, and they typically shake their heads rapidly from side-to-side when hooked in an often successful attempt to saw the leader. Fluorocarbon lets you bump up your leader size to counter this and have a shot at landing a large trout that you might have had to use lighter mono in order to trick in the first place.

If all of this fly fishing business is just too much to swallow for the casual angler, then rest assured that you can also have your own share of success with a handful of the appropriate terminal tackle, a few jars of Power Bait and the proper light spinning outfit. ODFW regularly stocks Timothy with catchable-sized trout during the late spring and summer months, and the survival rate over the winter is good so that many larger "hold-over" trout are available for harvest. Fish a 2-3' leader with an egg sinker so that the Power Bait floats up off the bottom and you're in business. Berkley Gulp makes a bait paste called Chunky Cheese that absolutely kills the stocked trout up here and elsewhere. Early in the season when the water is cold and the fish are cruising near the surface, fishing a pinch of night crawler or crawdad tail under a float can be especially effective.

There are few creatures in nature as pretty as the brook trout. Photo by Robert Campbell

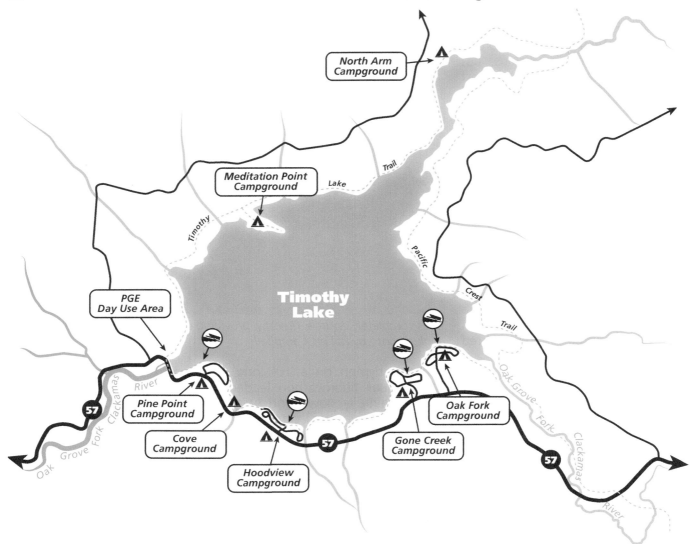

Casting lures is another good bet, especially early in the season, and spoons can be particularly deadly for torpid brook trout just waking up from a long winter. Cast the spoon adjacent to cover like stumps and weed beds and slowly reel in, although sometimes you can trigger a strike by speeding and slowing the retrieve in an erratic fashion to imitate a panicked, fleeing baitfish. Maintain a fairly tight line while the spoon is sinking so that you can feel any strikes that occur. Brook trout in particular often nail a spoon while it's sinking. The Acme Kamlooper and Kastmaster are particularly effective spoons at Timothy. The venerable Rooster Tail spinner from Worden's Tackle is also a killer at Timothy. I've done best on it in the natural colors like black, brown and green.

If you are going to troll for trout at Timothy, the best advice I can give if you are targeting the larger trout is to lose the lake troll or flasher. These devices, while effective for kokanee and planter trout, just seem to spook off the bigger fish. Though it seems counterintuitive, especially on a big lake like Timothy, try trolling just a small lure behind the boat like a F4 or F5 Worden's Flatfish, a size 50, 60 or 70 Luhr Jensen Hotshot, or a Frisky Fly. Trust me, the trout will see it. Use as little weight as possible to keep the lure fishing 5-10 feet below the surface and hang on! There are massive numbers of trout in Timothy, and if you find a productive area, you won't be able to troll very far between strikes. Light-bodied trolling spoons like the Worden's Triple Teaser, Luhr Jensen

Needlefish and Dick Nite are also effective at Timothy. Whatever lure you employ at Timothy, just be sure to troll as slowly as the lure style will allow you to for best results.

Besides the trout, there is an enormous population of kokanee at Timothy Lake. Largely viewed as plankton-eaters, kokanee at Timothy are also insectivorous and if you fly fish you will often catch them on midge pupa and mayfly nymphs. I've even caught a few of them on woolly buggers. I've witnessed kokanee feeding on the surface in such numbers during evening midge hatches that their rise rings made it look like it was raining when it was not. While kokanee are present in huge numbers in Timothy, these little salmon are small in size, even for kokanee. Timothy kokes typically

Black Metallic Bugger
Tied by Joe Warren

From crappie to carp to coho, buggers are the most versatile of patterns. Here's an attractor with profile, bugginess and flash. Swing it for steelhead, strip it for trout or shake it for smallmouth bass. Tier and originator, Joe Warren calls the Black Metallic Bugger his 'go-to' fly.

Change colors and sizes, especially the bead color to add variety or match local conditions. For a deeper drift, add a metal cone, a bead head or dumbbell eyes.

Tie this pattern with black thread on a No. 4-8XL Daiichi. For the tail, use a ¼-inch stub of black polypro yarn then add a hook-length of black fox with two strands of Flashabou. Tie in 2-pound monofilament and a black hackle feather. Wrap thread forward. Wrap hackle forward and secure with thread, whip finish and cut thread. Wrap mono over hackle and push a 3/0 gun metal glass bead back as tight as possible to hackle. Bring mono underneath the bead and make several wraps in front of it. Add another black hackle, wrap several times and tie off with mono then push a bead back, bringing the mono in front of the bead. Continue this pattern to the head and finish.

Cutthroat trout are native to the upper Clackamas drainage and therefore Timothy Lake. Many anglers choose to release them and bonk brook trout and rainbows instead. Photo by Robert Campbell

The variety of trout at Timothy will keep dedicated trout anglers searching for that next photo-op. Photo by Robert Campbell

measure from 7-10 inches on average, and a 12-incher would be a monster. Some say that it's an overpopulation problem that has stunted the kokanee at Timothy, while I've also heard it said that it has to do with the particular strain used for the original plant. Whatever the case may be, there are bazillions of these delicious little fish swimming around Timothy, and in a failed attempt to control their numbers, ODFW has for years allowed a generous 25-fish limit on kokanee in addition to other trout catch limits. Good thing, too, for it would take about that many to make a meal.

Timothy Lake is also famous for its delicious crawdads, and while the average size of these crustaceans seems to have dropped over the years, the lake is still stuffed with them. Bring a couple of traps up with you to soak while you fish for trout or kokanee, and you will have a nice side dish to compliment your evening meal back in camp. Or, for a bit of fun with the kids, wait until nightfall and wade the shallows with a flashlight and try to catch these snappy little critters by hand as they come out for their evening forays into the shallows.

Timothy is a giant body of water and it can be a little intimidating for the first-time angler to try and figure out where to fish. As previously mentioned, it is advisable to target trout near to the shoreline and if you try a particular area without any luck for an hour or so, pick up and move. Some of my favorite areas over the years are the the the cove where Dinger Creek flows in just north of the dam, the shoreline around Meditation Point, and the south shoreline between Pine Point Campground and the dam. This latter area, in fact, seems to be a magnet for large native rainbows in early spring just after the spawn. It is fairly common to catch lots of 14-20 inch here as soon as the lake is accessible in the spring. However, many of them are dark, emaciated fish with mushy flesh that would be terrible

Timothy Lake has many coves, bays and inlets that are perfect for smaller craft like float tubes and pontoon boats. Photo by Robert Campbell

to eat. If you catch any of these thin, dark-colored fish that look like little spawned-out steelhead, let them go to recover from the spawn and catch some firmer fish to eat.

There are also some nice shallows with stumps and brook trout located near Hoodview and Gone Creek Campgrounds. The arm where the Oak Grove Fork of the Clackamas River enters the lake can also be a very productive part of the lake for both trout and crawdads. There is also an excellent hatch of Hexagenia Mayflies in this part of the lake beginning around the first of July, but they hatch right at dark, so be mindful to the regulation that you are only allowed to trout fish in Oregon for one hour past legal sunset on any given day. These giant, yellow mayflies are a spectacle to behold and often drive the trout crazy as the surface of the lake boils with slashing trout.

On one Father's Day my brother Will and I took our dad to Timothy for old time's sake and we trolled the shoreline from the Oak Grove Fork Campground to the North Arm and back. We trolled within 20 feet or so of the shoreline around the lake pulling F4 Frog Flatfish

with a couple of split shot and 6-pound SeaGuar fluorocarbon leader to help keep our lures down (fluorocarbon sinks). In the few hours that we fished, we must have caught and released 100-plus trout—we just could not keep them off—including some very nice rainbows and brookies in the 14-20 inch range. That's Timothy Lake for you: hit it on the right day with the right technique, and you'll swear that you're on a Century Drive Lake near Bend and not some reservoir near Portland.

Directions: From Government Camp, head east on Highway 26 for approximately 11 miles before turning right (west) onto Skyline Road (Forest Rd. #42). Follow Skyline for about 7 miles to the Joe Graham Campground near Clackamas Meadow, and take Forest Road #57 the remaining 2 miles to the lake. An alternate route is to follow Highway 224 up the Clackamas River from Estacada to Ripplebrook, then take Road #57 which follows the Oak Grove Fork of the Clackamas River up to the dam. While this route is shorter in miles from the Portland area, it does take longer than cruising up Highway 26.

There are some wild rainbows in Timothy that can take you into your backing. Photo by Robert Campbell

Trillium Lake

Size	57 acres
Depth	16 feet
Trail	Circles lake
Difficulty	Wheelchair accessible
Elevation	3601 feet
GPS Coordinates:	N 45 15.556 W 121 33.561

Species: Rainbow, cutthroat, brook

Best Methods: Fly, still-fishing

Tips: Great place for a float tube.

For the iconic view of the mountain reflected in water, try Trillium Lake. This place is a favorite of many Portland-area anglers. Rainbows here average 8 to 14 inches. Cutthroat trout and brook trout are also found in Trillium. The Department of Fish and Wildlife stocks this lake throughout the season with plenty of trout to keep anglers happy. Larger fish are planted in August and September. Rainbows that winter over can tip the scales at 3 pounds by spring. With two launches, the boat access is good. No motors are allowed on Trillium.

Bank anglers find the best fishing on the south and eastern shores near the campground and day use area. A handicapped accessible fishing pier is very popular. Most anglers favor Power Bait, worms or salmon eggs. Rooster Tail or Promise Keeper spinners can be very effective. Try a frog-pattern spinner or spoon.

Floats keep baits out of the long grass and weeds. When fishing with jar baits, use a four- or five-foot leader.

This well-loved lake boasts gorgeous mountain views and fast fishing. To time it right, head to Trillium in the fall.
Photo by Pete Chadwell

Fly fishermen can catch trout from the bank, but the best bet is to take to the water in a float tube or small boat. In the absence of surface activity, wind drift with a slow-sink fly line and a tandem rig or use an indicator and chironomid setup.

For the biggest fish, hit Trillium when the snow melts and again at the end of the season. This lake is abused, especially in late June and early July. By September it is nearly forgotten except by those who know that the fishing can be very good in the fall.

Directions:

From Highway 26, drive east past Government Camp and look for the sign on the south side of the road. Follow the Trillium Lake Road two miles to the lake.

Dragonfly Nymph
Tied by Pete Ouellette

When stillwater trout are keying on dry dragonflies, the action can be fast and frustrating. Instead of fishing dry, tie on a Dragonfly Nymph and work it with a long leader on a floating line.

Fish this pattern slow with about a dozen short strips then make a long strip to simulate a "kill" which suggests the feeding action of the dragonfly nymph. Sometimes a trout will slam the bug to stun it then circle around to eat it.

Tie this Dragonfly Nymph pattern on a long shank No. 8 hook. For the tail, use three short goose biots. Build the body with mixed dark brown and olive wool. Rib with fluorescent green.

Resources

Nearest cities/towns:
Government Camp

Camping:
Trillium Lake Campground

Tackle:
Top Stop Food & Fuel

Visitor information:
Mt. Hood Area Chamber
www.mthood.org
503-622-3017

Pete Chadwell fishes the evening hatch at Trillium Lake. A black leech pattern is a great searching fly for evenings at Trillium. Photo by Gary Lewis

Photo by Matthew McFarland

Veda Lake

Size ....3 acres

Depth .... 12 feet

Trail ....Trailhead at Fir Tree Campground Rd. #2613

Difficulty ....Just under 3 miles round trip

Elevation .... 4,600 feet

Species: Brook trout, Crawdads

Best Methods: Spoons and spinners, night crawlers, fly fishing

Tips: Fly fishing is difficult from the shore, so bring a float tube

Veda Lake is a gorgeous little gem that rarely gets crowded despite its relative nearness to a state highway. Perhaps this is due to the fact that the last 3.5 miles in on Sherar Burn Road are tortuous. The road bed is comprised of jagged, rubber-eating rocks and nasty ruts that require extremely slow speed in order to avoid shredded tires, or worse. You should plan on it taking nearly an hour to cover this distance without damaging your vehicle. Yes, you could probably walk it faster. We've seen people make it to the trailhead in passenger vehicles, but a truck or jeep is advisable.

Veda was first stocked with trout in 1917 by a couple of guys named Vern and David who packed the trout fry in on their backs, and the story goes that the lake was named by combining the first two letters of their names. The hike in is fairly steep for the first half mile as you climb the flank of Veda Butte. When you reach the top the trail is more level for about a quarter mile before you begin the descent into the lake. This bench is a shining example of what a mixed old-growth forest should be, with a nice variety of trees growing here dominated by Noble Fir, Larch,

Fantastic dry fly fishing for brook trout is the draw at Veda Lake. Photo by Robert Campbell

Mountain Hemlock and Vine Maple. On the hike in watch for a unique fir that has four trunks growing from a single root system. It's on the right side of the trail near a switchback.

If you are fortunate to make this hike during clear weather, you will want to stop at several of the off-trail overlooks on the way down the hill. Be sure to keep a close watch over pets or children if you do, as there are no safety rails here to protect them from a fall. The view of Mt. Hood beyond the Still Creek watershed is magnificent from these vantage points. Wild flowers are plentiful here on the forest margins, with Bear Grass, Paintbrush, Lupine, Bearded Tongue and Cascade Lily being common.

Once at the lake, you will find very eager brook trout which are stocked by helicopter every couple of years. The average size varies each year, but expect trout mostly in the 6-10 inch range. Anything larger would be a trophy up here. But what they lack in size they make up for in eagerness and sheer beauty. Brook trout are gorgeous! One almost feels guilty frying them in sizzling butter—almost, because brook trout are also delicious.

With a short growing season at this elevation, the fish are cooperative most of the summer, though extended hot weather may slow the mid-day bite and find trout activity condensed into the early morning or evening hours. Early season access varies on the calendar each year according to snow pack, so make sure to check at the Zig Zag Ranger Station (503-622-3191) before heading out.

If you arrive to Veda while there are still snow banks melting away back in the trees, you will find its trout willing to smack just about anything, and this is when hardware like spinners and spoons really shines. A ¼ oz Acme Kastmaster in Brook Trout finish is hard to beat. A pinch of worm or crawdad tail fished under a float is also deadly this time of year.

Fly anglers will enjoy watching the trout jump out of the water to take mayflies from mid-air almost as much as they marvel at how little time there is between strikes on their own dry fly. If you like catching trout on the surface on light gear, Veda is the place for you. The trout in Veda seem enamored of taking flies off the top, and they will surprise you with their acrobatic maneuvers. This is a great place to break out your three-weight and enjoy a day catching several dozen trout in a quiet, forested setting.

The trout at Veda are not usually picky except for the size of bug, and just about any dry fly size 12 or smaller is going to get hammered, though sparse parachute types and adult midge patterns really shine up here. Of course, this rule goes out the window if ants are on the water. Bring a float tube for better access and much easier fly casting. Kicking along and casting to shoreline structure is deadly-effective. There are some large crawdads here if you're willing to carry in the trap, but please don't take more than dinner if you want to help conserve the population.

There are a couple of unimproved campsites here but no facilities; you'll have to pack in your own water or have a reliable filtration system. No trace camping techniques are advised. There is a fisherman's trail around the lake. Be forewarned that during the height of summer black flies and deer flies can be such a menace as to ruin the trip for the timid, and no amount of DEET seems to deter them, though they don't seem to bother you as much when you're out on the water. Here's yet another reason to pack in a float tube.

Directions

Follow U.S. Highway 26 east of Government Camp and shortly after the summit turn into Still Creek Campground. Drive through the campground—slowly—and go about a mile to the second road on the right, East Chimney Rock Road. Follow this for about a half mile to a four-way intersection and continue south on Sherar Burn Road (#2613) for 3.5 miles to the trailhead at Fir Tree Campground. Nearby attractions include Summit Meadow, where pioneers on the last leg of The Oregon Trail camped and pastured their stock. Also nearby are the Pioneer Graves, where sadly for several people the trail ended.

Resources

Nearest cities/towns:
Government Camp

Camping:
Trillium Lake Campground

Tackle:
Top Stop Food & Fuel

Visitor information:
Mt. Hood Area Chamber
www.mthood.org
503-622-3017

Hood River

Length	25 miles
Regulations	Artificial fly & lure
Elevation at mouth	80 feet

Species: Cutthroat, rainbow, steelhead, coho, chinook, bull trout

Best Methods: Fly, spinner

Tips: Watch fish counts at Bonneville Dam for steelhead and salmon timing

Robert Campbell caught this Hood River steelhead on a Gorman Egg Pattern from Umpqua Feather Merchants, a pattern that is deadly on steelhead just about everywhere. Photo by Robert Campbell.

On the old maps, this freestone river was called Dog River. Before that, Lewis and Clark called it the Labeasche River, named for one of the members of the expedition. But the name Hood River began to be applied in the late 1850s and the name stuck.

The river originates in the Ladd Glacier (West Fork), Coe and Eliot glaciers (Middle Fork) and the Newton-Clark Glacier (East Fork) on the east and north sides of Mount Hood. The Hood and its tributaries drain some of the most beautiful country east of the Cascades, from the mountains to the pastoral apple orchards and croplands surrounding the communities of Parkdale, Dee, Odell, and the town of Hood River.

Long rapids and fast-flowing pools are characteristic of this stream. Native rainbows and cutthroat can be found throughout most of the river while steelhead, chinook and coho can be found in the lower reaches.

In 2010, the Powerdale Dam was removed and 120 miles of wild stream spawning habitat was opened to natural fish passage for the first time in more than 100 years.

Steelhead and salmon fishing is open in the mainstem Hood River up to the deadline at Punchbowl

Falls. Anglers may keep adipose fin-clipped coho and steelhead all year. Use of bait is allowed for salmon and steelhead all the way up to confluence with the West Fork. Regulations are subject to change. Check the current Oregon Sport Fishing Regulations prior to fishing.

Fly-fishing is popular and effective. Deep in the canyon, the river does not have the sun on the water as long as in some other streams, so an angler armed with a single-hand rod or a two-hander can entice steelhead to take a bug on the swing, whether chugged on the surface or behind a sink-tip. When the sun is on the water, a beadhead nymph and indicator presentation is usually more effective.

Steelhead and silvers can be taken on spinners too. The best water is broken at the surface and runs at the speed of a fast walk. It is easy to rig for spinner fishing, just tie on a spinner - minimum eight-pound test - and cast it. A slow retrieve is way more enticing than a fast crank. Try to work the deeper reaches of holes.

Another good bet is to use a float and a marabou jig. Rig the jig to ride about 18 inches above the bottom to put the lure in front of the nose of holding fish. For steelhead, use black, blue, purple and green. The best coho colors are chartreuse, red, purple and pink.

Trout fishing is open, catch-and-release only, from the May river opener through the end of October. When fishing the upper reaches for native trout, ply the seams adjacent to the riffles where trout have to expend less energy to survive. Ledges and rock overhangs offer cover to the bigger trout. Fish these spots for a chance at catching a predator waiting

Jason Hambly of Lamiglas Fishing Rods caught this small but beautiful Hood River spring chinook on a spinner. Photo by Robert Campbell.

for the river to bring him insects and unwary baitfish.

Small spinners and spoons in brass, black, and brown are effective. Fly fishermen should drift small stonefly and caddis patterns or try attractor dry flies like the Royal Wulff, the Irresistible and the various Humpy patterns.

When prospecting for bigger trout, try swinging sculpin patterns. Fish them on a five- to six-foot leader with a tight line, making them swim and scoot along the bottom.

Bull trout, whose populations are considered threatened, are present in both the Clear Branch and the mainstem Hood River. Bull trout are char and can be identified by light pink and yellow spots against a darker olive background. Because bull trout are predators and make their living eating other fish, they are more likely to be caught on a swinging or sculpin presentation.

When fly-fishing or spinning for trout, it's a good idea to pinch the barbs on the hooks. Try to keep the fish in the water during the release. Take a picture and let it go.

To fish the lower river, access it from Highway 84 at the town of Hood River. Highway 35 runs parallel to the lower river for the first four miles. Take the Hood River Highway to follow the mainstem Hood as far upstream as the town of Trout Creek.

Directions

The West Fork of the Hood River and its tributaries and the Clear Branch and Pinnacle Creek are closed to angling to protect spawning trout, salmon, and steelhead. For information on the East Fork, turn to the East Fork Hood River chapter.

Purple Steelhead Muddler
Courtesy Confluence Fly Shop

For the pinnacle of steelhead fishing excitement, tease the fish up to the surface with a waking fly. Watch for the bulge when the fish charges. At the take, let it turn and pull line before you lift the rod. The Steelhead Muddler is tied sparse to run at the surface and just beneath it. Use a floating line and throw a high mend to slow the fly's progress.

If a fish follows but does not take, make a step back upstream and throw the same cast. If it refuses again, tie on a smaller fly and swing it through the same water.

Tie the Steelhead Muddler on a No. 6 up-eye steelhead dry fly hook. For the body, use purple mylar. Tie in an underwing of dyed purple squirrel tail. Then tie in a dyed purple turkey quill. At the collar, wrap and spin clumps of deer hair. To finish, trim a bullet-shaped head.

Resources

Nearest cities/towns:
Parkdale, Hood River

Camping:
Hood River Ranger District

Tackle:
The Fly Fishing Shop, Welches
www.flyfishusa.com

Gorge Fly Shop

Visitor information:
Hood River Chamber of Commerce
www.mthood.org
800-366-3530

East Fork Hood River

Length	15 miles
Regulations	Artificial fly & lure
	Catch & Release
Trail	Follows the river
Elevation at mouth	80 feet

Species: Rainbow trout

Best Methods: Fly, spinner

Tips: Check streamside boulders and rocks for insects and try to match the hatch

Fed from snowmelt from the Newton-Clark Glacier, the East Fork flows north into the Upper Hood River Valley. This pretty freestone tributary of the Hood River is 15 miles long and is managed for its population of wild rainbows and cutthroat.

Two of the East Fork's important tributaries are the Middle Fork Hood River and the Dog River, a name which recalls a starving pioneer party that had to resort to eating dogs to survive the Oregon Trail.

For many years the river was stocked with hatchery rainbows, but that practice has ended and now the East Fork is a great place to search out wild trout with a fly rod or an ultralight rigged with fly or lure.

When last we fished the East Fork, we caught cutthroats and cutt-bows on dry flies when the sun was low in the sky. Toward lunch time, the fish seemed more reluctant to come to the surface so we switched to stonefly imitations and caught a few more, including our biggest trout of the day.

In the upper reaches of the East Fork, the trout average six to seven inches in length. Downstream the river runs richer with food and the trout run a little larger. Don't expect to catch a lot of big ones. Here, a ten-incher is a real trophy, although there are bigger trout that haunt the deepest holes and make their living on mayflies, stoneflies and small fry.

Stock the fly box with a selection of dries: Parachute Adams, Purple Haze, Royal Wulff, Blue Winged Olive, Humpy, Stimulator and Black Gnat. With the exception of the Stimulator, the most productive flies will be sized No. 14s and No. 16s. When the fish are feeding subsurface, drift a No. 10 beadhead stonefly nymph with a No. 14 Lightning Bug or similar beadhead nymph.

To rig a spinning rod, spool up with six-pound test mainline and a plastic float and a red-tag Woolly Worm or any of the above-mentioned flies on a 4-pound test leader. To prospect under log jams tie on a very small Flatfish and work it down in fast

The East Fork's native cutts and rainbows are eager to take a dry. For bigger trout, try to get away from the road.
Photo by Gary Lewis

water. In larger pools, switch to a small spinner like a black Rooster Tail or one of Mack's Lure's small Promise Keepers. Cast and crank it back, making sure that the blade is spinning.

Because the East Fork is a catch-and-release fishery, please pinch down the barbs on all hooks.

This is a classic wet-wading stream. Unless it's a really cold day, leave the waders in the car and step in to the water in your hiking boots. There are fish in most of the runs, but the more distance between the parking area and the water, the easier they are to catch. And the biggest will be found in the deepest, darkest water.

Directions

Find the East Fork by following Highway 35 north from Highway 26. Look for the crossing of the White River and then the East Fork. After a few miles the road crosses the river again. The road follows the river for approximately 12 miles. Try Robinhood campground or Sherwood campground in this stretch.

Tommy Brown drifts a dry fly through a riffle on the East Fork. Photo by Gary Lewis

The March Brown is a classic that has stood the test of time. Tied to represent a mayfly, its wings are durable and it rides high on the surface. Courtesy The Patient Angler

These sub-alpine salmonids have a look all their own. Photo by Gary Lewis

Resources

Nearest cities/towns:
Parkdale, Hood River

Camping:
Hood River Ranger District

Tackle:
The Fly Fishing Shop, Welches
www.flyfishusa.com

Gorge Fly Shop

Visitor information:
Hood River Chamber of Commerce
www.mthood.org
800-366-3530

White River

Length	50 miles
Trail	Difficult
Regulations	Artificial fly & lure
Depth	2 to 5 feet

Species: Rainbow trout

Best Methods: Fly fishing

Tips: Fish early in the season, through June

It begins in the White River glacier, in eastern Hood River County. The headwaters are in a steep canyon between Timberline Lodge and Mount Hood Meadows. From there it flows southeast for roughly 12 miles then turns southeast for about eight miles then trends east and north past Tygh Valley to its confluence with the Deschutes, north of Maupin.

The river's name comes from the color of the glacial water and it is often ignored by anglers who are used to water they can see into. Other factors that limit angler attention are the distance of the stream from population centers, a high percentage of private land ownership along the lower river and the rugged terrain.

The river runs through a deep canyon after leaving the Mt. Hood National Forest. Groves of oak and pine give shade to the deer, elk, bear, wild turkeys and gray squirrels that take their water from the stream.

Rapids, pools and tailouts are characteristic of this stream that loses so much elevation in 50 miles. Almost every year, in August or September, a piece of the glacier that feeds the river breaks off and the river will run high and muddy for up to three weeks.

Fish can be found throughout most of the river, from the point where it is crossed by Highway 35 down to its confluence with the Deschutes. Rainbow trout are the predominant species. In the upper river, as in the upper reaches of most mountain streams, fish are small. Catch a 12-incher and you've landed a trophy. With more food at the lower elevation, the rainbows run to 15 inches in the middle river and can get much, much bigger. Three falls in the last three miles of river divide the trout population.

Steelhead can be found in the lower river, and all rainbows over 20 inches in length are considered steelhead. All non-finclipped steelhead must be released unharmed.

Fishermen are restricted to angling with artificial lures and flies throughout the river. Downstream from the lowest falls, the fishing is regulated by Deschutes River section 1 rules. Fish early and late

Don Lewis fishes fast water on the White River. The river's name comes from the color of the glacial water.
Photo by Gary Lewis

in the day for the best success. During the day, try the shaded, deeper water. Look for the biggest fish in the slower water where trout have to expend less energy to survive.

With a gravel bottom and some silting in the lower river, the White River may be waded throughout most of its length. Cast brown, black and orange Rooster Tail spinners in the lower and middle river. Use flies from the headwaters to the mouth.

Visibility in the water is low throughout the year, but dry flies do bring fish to the surface. Try a Purple Parachute Adams when mayflies are on the water. Be ready to match caddis hatches in late May and June.

One of the most effective techniques for the White River is nymphing with bead head flies like the No. 12-16 Spitfire, Prince Nymph, Hot Spot Pheasant Tail, Blue Beadhead Copper or Silver Lightning Bug. To get the fly down where fish will eat it, tie the small nymph on 12 to 18 inches of leader and knot it to a large stonefly nymph like a No. 6 Black Western Stone or a No. 8-10 Golden Epoxyback Stone. Tungsten bead flies, though more expensive, will sink faster in the water column. Use a strike indicator positioned about twice the depth of the current to keep the flies drifting at the proper depth in riffled water.

Weighted crayfish imitations and baitfish patterns are also effective. Fish them on a shorter leader with a tight line, making them swim and scoot along the bottom.

Directions

To fish the upper White River, leave Highway 26 and head north on Highway 35 to the river. Take Forest Road 48 south to the Barlow Road Crossing. From Barlow Crossing, Forest Road 3530 follows the west side of the river for approximately four miles.

To find the lower river, take Highway 216 then turn left between Wapinitia and Pine Grove. Or, take Highway 197 to the bridge east of Tygh Valley where it crosses the river.

Resources

Nearest cities/towns:

Parkdale, Hood River

Camping:

Hood River Ranger District

Tackle:

The Fly Fishing Shop, Welches
www.flyfishusa.com
Gorge Fly Shop

Visitor information:

Hood River Chamber of Commerce
www.mthood.org
800-366-3530

Gary Lewis shows off an apple cobbler prepared over the coals in a Camp Chef Dutch oven. Photo by Gary Lewis

Around the fire anticipating the next day's hike and fishing. Photo by Gary Lewis

Deschutes River
Pelton Dam to the Columbia

Length................................. 252 miles

Regulations..................... Artificial fly & lure

Elevation at source .... 4,474 feet

Elevation at Warm Springs ..... 1,539 feet

Elevation at Maupin.................. 1,047 feet

Elevation at mouth........................ 164 feet

Species: Rainbow, bull trout, steelhead, coho, chinook, sockeye, whitefish, and pikeminnow

Best Methods: Fly fishing, spin-fishing

It is by turns accessible and remote, urbanized and wild; a river of contrasts. Where the water spills out of Little Lava Lake, it is not much more than a creek, while 200 miles downstream, the Deschutes River becomes the archetype of the great Western river.

The Deschutes flows right through Bend, the biggest city east of the Cascades, where people that love the river can behold it every day of the year. But to know it, an angler must fish it in all its moods, at its headwaters, in the rattlesnake-infested canyons, in its reservoirs and its pocket water. It is democratic too, offering something for every angler, from predatory browns and bull trout to wild rainbows that sip caddis by the hundreds in June to steelhead and salmon in September.

The river gathers its water from the Cascades and from the high desert as it flows south to the Columbia. About 83 river miles up from the mouth, the Warm Springs River joins the Deschutes and downstream near Tygh Valley, the glacial-tinged White River spills in.

This section of river, below Pelton Dam is considered the lower Deschutes and though the land ownership might seem a bit complex to the newcomer, the Deschutes is easy to access even in some of the best fishing water.

The Warm Springs tribes own and controls the west bank of the river from 16 miles south of Maupin to Lake Billy Chinook and up to the mouth of Jefferson Creek on the Metolius River arm. Non-tribal members are allowed access to six miles of reservation land at Dry Creek. A tribal permit is required and may be purchased in Madras and in Warm Springs.

On the east bank, drive-to and walk-in access can

For fresh summer steelhead, hit the river in September. Photo by Robert Campbell

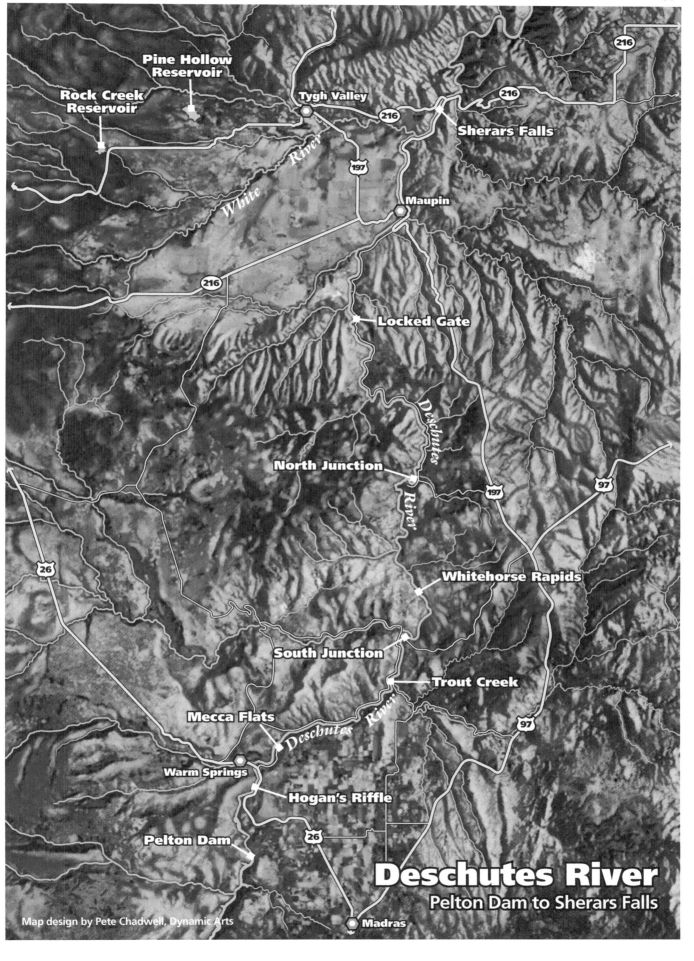

Pine Hollow Reservoir

Rock Creek Reservoir

Tygh Valley

216

216

Sherars Falls

White River

197

Maupin

216

Locked Gate

Deschutes River

North Junction

197

97

Whitehorse Rapids

South Junction

Trout Creek

97

Mecca Flats

Deschutes River

26

Warm Springs

Hogan's Riffle

Pelton Dam

26

Deschutes River
Pelton Dam to Sherars Falls

Madras

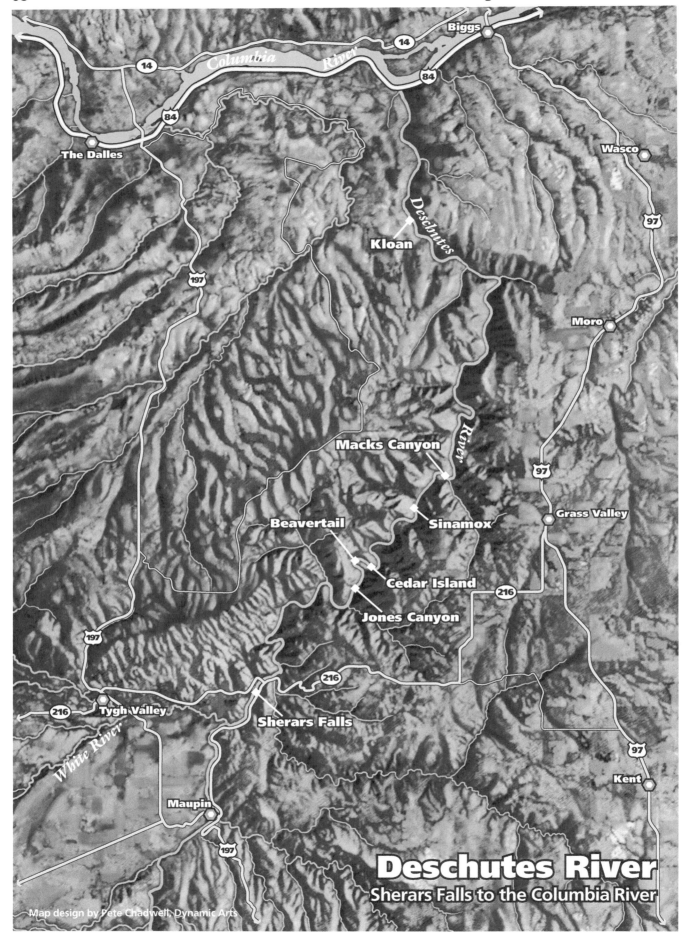

Map design by Pete Chadwell, Dynamic Arts

Deschutes River
Sherars Falls to the Columbia River

Sherar's Falls is one of the most powerful rapids in the West. Just downstream in the oxygenated water, steelhead and salmon rest before making the run up through the falls. Photo by Gary Lewis

be found upstream from the launch at Warm Springs where Highway 26 follows the river.

Downstream from the bridge at Warm Springs, on the east side of the river, bank anglers can find Upper Mecca and Lower Mecca, just upstream from the mouth of Dry Creek on the opposite side of the river. This section of river is usually referred to as the Warm Springs to Trout Creek drift and can be drifted in just a few hours with a shuttle and take-out at the Trout Creek ramp. Good bank access can also be found at Trout Creek and again at South Junction. The road doesn't come down to the east side of the river again until Maupin.

On the river, this section is called Trout Creek to Maupin, and requires a multi-day float and should only be attempted by experienced boaters. This is the stretch of river that contains the White Horse rapids, which claims many boats each year. White Horse should be scouted before each run. Campsites in the lower river are managed by the Bureau of Land Management and boaters' passes are required (see Resources sidebar).

Highway 197 crosses the river at Maupin and it's here the traveling angler can find miles of river to explore. The river is most accessible from the east bank and a good road follows down from town to Sherar's Falls and beyond. In the summer, this section is popular with rafters, who put in at Wapinitia Rapids upstream and drift down to a takeout called Sandy Beach, just above Sherar's Falls. Sherar's Falls should be witnessed, but from the road, not from the seat of a boat. The rapids are considered un-navigable in any craft. Here, just below the falls, the Warm Springs tribes practice their dip-netting from wooden platforms built out over the river.

At Sherar's Bridge, Highway 216

Resources

Permits:

Deschutes River Boater Pass
541-416-6700
www.boaterpass.com

Tribal Fishing Permits
541-553-2042
www.tribalpermit.com

Bend/Redmond/ Sisters Area

Nearest cities/towns:
Bend, Redmond, Sisters, Sunriver

Tackle:
Confluence Fly Shop
www.confluenceflyshop.com

Fin and Fire
www.finandfire.com

The Fly Fisher's Place
www.flyfishersplace.com

Fly and Field Outfitters
www.flyandfield.com

The Hook Fly Shop
www.hookfish.com

Patient Angler Fly Shop
www.patientangler.com

Stillwater Fly Shop
www.stillwaterflyshop.com

Sunriver Fly Shop
www.sunriverflyshop.com

Fisherman's Marine manager LeAnn Reardon about to release a wild steelhead she caught fishing with über guide Brad Staples. Photo by Robert Campbell

crosses the river and access can be found on both banks. This is a popular place for salmon fishermen in the years when the river opens for either spring chinook or fall salmon. The fish stack in the fast water below the falls.

Another option for the bank angler is to drive up from Maupin to the locked gate, imaginatively called the Locked Gate. This is private land and access is allowed for day trips with fly rods and/or spinning rods.

Headed downstream, the road continues down from Sherar's Falls to Pine Tree, the beginning of a popular float called Pine Tree to Mack's Canyon that can be accomplished in a one-day (or stretch it out and fish two days) drift to Mack's Canyon. Another option is to put in at Mack's and float out to Moody Rapids (the last rapids on the river), typically called the Mack's to the Mouth float.

A hiking trail follows the river down from Mack's Canyon while the railroad tracks hug the western bank.

The next drive-in access is at Kloan where the road goes all the way down to a parking area. Some people call it a road. Other people call it a cliff. The prudent park up on top and walk down (and back up at the end of the day). Want to test your towing insurance? Drive down to the river.

For access at the mouth of the river drive to Biggs on Highway 97 or Interstate 84 and follow the signs to west to the Deschutes. Deschutes River State Park is located on the east bank of the river and offers camping and day use facilities. The boat ramp is located on the west bank of the river at Heritage Landing. Good trails lead up both sides of the river and anglers can go in on foot, astride a mountain bike or even on horseback. Watch for rattlesnakes.

Flyfishing for Deschutes Redsides

For the trout fisherman on the Deschutes, the New Year starts with the appearance of the first salmonfly on the wing. It happens sometime in late April when the water warms and old Pteronarcys migrates to shore, crawls out on the bank and dries his wings. This is a bug that can stretch a tape measure to over two inches and should be matched with a fly tied on an extra long No. 4 dry fly hook. Almost concurrent with the salmonfly hatch is the golden stone, which is nearly as big (Nos. 6-10). The migration stirs the tastebuds of the trout and big rainbows begin to take up stations close to the bank. At the height of the hatch, clouds of salmonflies and golden stoneflies can be seen above the river and in the tall grass along the water.

The best salmonfly and golden stonefly patterns seem to change from year to year. Definitely carry a selection in various sizes, in both orange and yellow. Start with Whitlock's Adult Stonefly, Egg-Laying Stonefly, Spencer's Chewy Stone and Rainy's Orange Gorilla Stonefly. And definitely stop in at a local fly shop and get the latest scoop.

While the big bugs get the most attention, mayflies can turn a trout's head, if only for a taste of something a bit different. In April, May and June, March browns and baetis can be seen on the water. Green drake mayflies begin to show up in late May and these big mayflies are definitely a favorite of big rainbows.

Trout eat salmonflies and golden stones till they can't stand it anymore and, as the big stoneflies taper off, caddis flies become the main item on the menu. While the salmonfly hatch was on, most of the

action was close to shore. Now the fish spread out through the river again, as caddis flies could appear anywhere in the riffled water.

A well-stocked box should include a Hemingway Caddis, tan, olive and black Elk Hair Caddis and X-Fly Caddis. While dry flies can produce action anytime during the day, a caddis emerger may turn more fish. When there is no hatch in evidence, plan to fish nymphs. Beadhead nymphs are a good bet when they match what the fish are eating. Try turning over rocks or running a fine mesh net through the water to see what protein drifts with the current. When fishing beadheads, rig two in tandem and set a strike indicator at two times the depth in riffled water.

While watching for caddis, don't overlook the tiny tricos or pale morning dun mayflies. If the fish are being selective, it pays to size down and focus on casting to rising trout. To match these mayflies, tie or buy small Pale Morning Duns, Cripple PMDs, Purple Haze and Parachute Adams.

Caddis and mayfly hatches come and go through October. One of the best caddis hatches of the year may come off in the fall when the October caddis shed their cases and the pupa emerge to dry their wings and fly or die in the mouths of trout.

Midge hatches and blue-winged olive mayflies may come off at any time of the year. For midges, keep a selection of Hi-Viz Griffiths Gnats, Cheech's Black Bunny Midges and Swink's Bob. To match the blue-winged olives, use BWO Parachutes and CDC patterns.

In January and February look for a hatch of little black stoneflies. This can be matched with a black Elk Hair Caddis, but a black/orange Stimulator could be a better choice when tied down to a No. 14.

At various times of the year, an angler might encounter terrestrials on the water. Ants, hoppers and cricket patterns are good to keep in the dry fly box.

To target bigger fish, carry a selection of minnow imitations like a Conehead Muddler Minnow, Conehead White Bunny Muddler.

Resources *(Cont.)*

The Dalles Area

Nearest cities/towns:
Warm Springs, Maupin, The Dalles, Biggs

Tackle:
Flyfishing Strategies, Bi-Mart, Gorge Outfitters

Camping:
Deschutes River State Recreation Area, www.oregonstateparks.org

Visitor information:
The Dalles Chamber of Commerce
www.thedalleschamber.com
541-296-2231

November fishing can be fast and furious. Use a sink-tip to reach steelhead in the colder water.

Flyfishing for Deschutes Steelhead

Across the river, the last few cars of a freight train turned the corner and rattled out of sight down the twin steel rails. A few yellowed leaves rattled in the shoreside willows, a lone pine tree stood tall against a sky white with clouds.

With my box open, water swirling about my boots, I picked out a fly and knotted it to my 10-pound tippet. I waded in slow and shook line out of the long two-handed rod. This was small, quiet water, where the river flattens out on a turn, then runs out in a riffle.

I fished near shore first, in case there were fish close to the bank. Water burbled into the pool behind me. A steelhead rose on the seam of the riffle, her nose and tail broke the surface. I took another step down, cast again and boomed out a long quartering-down cast.

As the fly reached the terminus of the drift, I felt a subtle pull, dropped the tip, and pointed the rod at the fish. It tugged again. I lifted and the fish turned, raced

across the tailout and into the fast water below. Line peeled off the reel and tore into the backing as the nine-pound native hen turned a cartwheel, then blasted into the next riffle, like a freight train going downhill.

The path of the steelheader is not an easy road. The first few years, successful trips are few and far between. The steelhead is elusive, aloof, secretive and shy; he is tempestuous, arrogant, and acrobatic. On the fly, he is the Northwest's greatest fishing challenge.

To catch him, learn to read the water. Steelhead follow the path of least resistance, often an underwater path parallel to a bank or high cliff, often close to shore. Look for seams and foam lines, indicating the transitions of swift and slow water. Such places allow steelhead to travel with fewer obstacles.

Concentrate on fishing water that is two to six feet deep and moves at the speed of a fast walk. Pay particular attention to soft inside seams and slow tailouts.

You have to put the fly within the strike zone. In the winter, that strike zone is smaller and you need to go deeper to provoke a fish to follow and strike.

Depth, distance, leader length, knot and fly. They are all important, but not nearly as important as delivery. Here's where it all comes together, or falls apart. Make that downstream cast, throw the upstream mend and then let it swing.

If the cast is sloppy or the mend doesn't lift, don't try to fix it, just let it drift. At the end of the swing, let the fly hang downstream for a moment.

Most grabs come on the swing. From the time the fly splashes down to the time you lift it out of the water,

Salmonflies begin their migration toward shore in early May.

there could be a fish behind it. A rod twitch or a re-mend can move the fly up to six feet upstream in an erratic darting motion that might spook the chromer coming to crush your fly.

In the summer and early fall, fish are more likely to chase the fly. The winter bite is subtle. Often, steelhead will follow and peck at the fly as it swings. Don't try to set the hook. It's better to let the fish hook itself. All you need to do is lift the tip as the fish turns away.

The drag shrieks as the fish takes out your backing and cartwheels on the surface. In winter's slanted light, you lean into the current, focused, connected to a surging power.

The Deschutes River moves with a ponderous force, a single-minded purpose that we may harness for its energy, but never really tame. The stream, winding in and out of our collected history, gives up its silver-sided secrets to those who search them out with a swinging fly.

Resources *(Cont.)*

Maupin Area

Nearest cities/towns:
Warm Springs, Maupin, The Dalles, Biggs

Accommodations:
River Run Lodge, Imperial River Company, Oasis Resort

Tackle:
Deschutes Canyon Fly Shop, www.flyfishingdeschutes.com; Deschutes Angler Fly Shop, www.deschutesangler.com

Visitor information:
Maupin Area Chamber, www.maupinoregon.com, 541-993-1708; Maupin, www.cityofmaupin.com

Warm Springs Area Resources

Nearest cities/towns:
Warm Springs, Madras

Tackle:
The Flyfishing Shop, Welches www.flyfishusa.com

Accommodations:
Kah-Nee-Ta

Visitor information:
www.warmsprings.com

To see and do:
Kah-Nee-Ta, the Museum at Warm Springs

Columbia River
Bonneville Dam to The Dalles

Elevation at The Dalles	252 feet
Elevation at Hood River	160 feet
Depth	100 feet+

Species. Sturgeon, steelhead, coho, chinook, walleye, bass, shad, perch and more

Best Methods: Bait, casting, plunking

It is the great river of the West, the Columbia, a complex system, rich with opportunity for the angler. In the shadow of Mt. Hood, between Bonneville Dam and The Dalles, can be found one of the most productive reaches of the river for warmwater fish. Ocean-going species move through this section as well, and provide great sport during certain parts of the year. To time the best fishing for salmon, steelhead and shad, watch the counts on the Columbia dams fish passage reports available on the web. Because they are the biggest fish in the river, every angler should experience the sturgeon fishery at least once in their lifetimes.

Sturgeon: Down the river with a dinosaur

After an hour, the 80-pound line started to powder. That's what happens when the stress is so great, the line is almost at its breaking point. Little puffs of green popped from the mono and curly strands frayed like split ends on an aging rock star.

Erin Dauenhauer, who makes her living as a hairstylist, recommended a keratin treatment. I suggested Lee try to get a bit of line back and bury the damage on the spool.

On one end of the line there was a 400-pound sturgeon, on the other, a 180-pound firefighter, my friend Lee Sandberg. Minutes into the battle, the great beast ripped line around a rocky spire about 35 feet down. We saw it in the chatter of the rod.

At the helm, Greg Gustafson went into action and spun the boat back in the opposite direction to unwrap the fish from the rocks.

As soon as Sandberg felt the fish solid again, he put the backbone of the big Melton rod to its test. It would be an hour before we saw the beast of the fish that had taken a whole shad as the bait.

Now we followed the fish wherever it wanted to go and it mostly wanted to go downstream. We took turns, fighting the fish to an angry standstill alongside the boat.

Still we had not accomplished our goal. Erin had fought and lost one, had looked a ten-foot sturgeon in the eyeball when it leaped next to the boat, but we wanted one she could call hers. We even cut the bait down in hopes we'd hook a smaller one.

It had been what Gustafson called a slow day, a couple of hours of waiting, of re-baiting, of positioning in the current before the first fish, close to ten feet long, took the bait and began to streak away, throwing the hook at the top of a leap.

Gustafson prepared the baits which we found beneath the impatient beaks of seagulls. Shad are the main food source of the sturgeon, millions of the giant minnows streak upriver in May, June and July to cast their spawn on the water. The biomass creates a sturgeon feeding frenzy as the big fish follow them upstream.

Erin caught a shad in the dip net and minutes later it had a couple of half-hitches around it and a hook at the beak.

After Sandberg's sturgeon was released, we tied to the buoy again and slipped the baits into the current. Shadows began to lengthen and Mount Hood took on an orange glow.

The 23-year-old from Ashland stood on the gunnel and hung from the skeleton of the roof canopy. She dipped her toes in the water and watched the rod tip. Down in the mighty river, a beast followed a scent trail that bled out of an unfortunate shad.

Sometimes the smallest fish make the rod tip shake a lot more than a big one will. A big sturgeon with a mouth like a garbage can will just park on the bait and that might translate to a trembling in the rod.

We saw that tremor and the 23-year-old tiptoed to the rod holder where she eased the rod out and

Fighting big fish is a team effort when the fish might weigh in at 400 pounds or more. Here Greg Gustafson watches while Lee Sandberg and Erin Dauenhauer release an eight-footer. Photo by Gary Lewis

then punched the big old fish with the hook set. Instead of jumping like the first two had done, this one blasted away. Sandberg strapped the fighting belt around her waist while I reeled in the other rod and Gustafson threw off the bow line. We'd follow the dinosaur down the river.

Before he'd caught his, Sandberg said his previous biggest fish had been a tuna, maybe 15 pounds. Now this was fish number four and the pair from southern Oregon had figured out how to fight them.

To battle the big ones, it takes the whole body. Wedge the toes in the gunwale, seat the rod butt below the belt, put a thumb on the spool, grasp the rod at the top of the handle, lean back, gain a little line, reel down and do it again. It worked muscles that the hairdresser didn't know she had. She'd gain ten feet of line, the fish would turn its head and pull out thirty.

It's hard to say how long that fish was, but at the boat, 40 minutes later, it looked most of nine feet, its gray and white body already swollen with shad.

As more of the food fish make it up to The Dalles and beyond through July and into August, the beasts will gather beneath the dams to feed on their carcasses. The wind turbines beat on the horizon and the great river's energy flows in harness through the dam and there is no better place to test one's own power than against the great dinosaur of the Columbia.

Sturgeon are opportunistic bottom feeders that follow the feed, rooting with their snouts and detecting morsels with their sensitive barbels. Find the feed and you will find the fish. Contrary to common belief, a sturgeon's eyesight is sharp, though it relies mainly on its excellent sense of smell to find a meal.

Freshwater clams, decaying flesh, lamprey larva, eggs, worms, crayfish, snails, and anything else that lives, grows, and dies on the bottom can be food for sturgeon. Columbia River fish travel up and down the river to find the best concentrations of food.

Little depressions in the river bottom concentrate the food as the current sweeps it downstream. A depth finder helps the fisherman find these hidden sturgeon kitchens. Look for places where the depth changes, little depressions ten to twenty feet deeper than the surrounding bottom. The exception is when sturgeon are feeding on clams which are usually found in flat beds.

When your depth finder locates the kitchen, look for the fish, then set up

Any day on the river an angler has a chance to catch a state record smallmouth or a new personal best. Terry Sheely has caught bigger smallmouth than this, but he really can't remember when. Photo by Gary Lewis

upstream to run your lines back to them. Often the fish finder will show other fish higher in the water column. Because of their smaller air bladders, sturgeon are harder to spot. Look for blips along the bottom. Use the 'zoom' feature on your depth finder to magnify the bottom.

The most important part of your tackle is the hook. Fishing regulations on the Columbia River require a barbless hook to facilitate a quick release. Use a 5/0-9/0 barbless single hook, tied on Dacron leaders. Tie up leaders in advance for quick replacement on the river. Leave the leader long until it is rigged with bait. When rigged, best leader lengths for sturgeon are six to fourteen inches, unless you're using whole shad for bait. When fishing with whole shad, use a longer leader. Leader length depends on the type and size of bait being used as well as how it is rigged. Use a longer leader if you half-hitch the bait and shorter if you thread the bait.

Use a sliding sinker rig to allow the fish to take the bait without feeling much resistance from the weight, but heavy enough to keep your bait on the bottom. This will change based on current and tidal influence. Sinkers should be rigged to slide freely using plastic tubing to protect your main line.

Bank anglers often choose

Much of the action for salmon focuses on the river closer to the ocean, but salmon like this big Chinook can be caught where they stack up at the mouths of tributaries. Photo by Steve Leonard

monofilament because it offers better abrasion resistance. Braided line is a good choice for the boat angler because it doesn't stretch and allows a quick hook set. Go to heavier line when fishing for oversize fish.

Sturgeon fishing regulations are in a constant state of evolution as scientists, fisheries managers, and fishermen learn more about these great fish. Take the time to read the current regulations before you fish.

Chaos, coho and kings on the Columbia

Forest fire smoke hung in the air, diffused the light and cast a haze over the river. An east wind blew down the gorge and riffled the water in wavelets that lapped against the boat.

There were 24 boats at the mouth of the White Salmon when we motored across the Columbia from Hood River. Dave Eng, of SalmonTroutSteelheader magazine, was our captain. He handed out Lamiglas rods with big line counter casting reels. Cindy Thompson and I took up stations at the back of the boat, while Doug Eckelkamp and Zack Scheidegger of Alps Mountaineering grabbed the forward seats.

It was day three of Fish Camp at Peach Beach on the Columbia, fishing for salmon, steelhead, walleye, bass and sturgeon while trying out new gear from Cabela's, Coast, Camp Chef, WorkSharp, Lamiglas and Izorline.

A quick glance showed a third of the boats were trolling, while most fished salmon roe. Hover-fishing, they call it. Drop bait to the bottom, then bring it up two cranks. Bounce it on the bottom and you will hook a sturgeon.

One couple was fishing with

Guide Lance Fisher runs the kicker during a battle with a king. Photo by Gary Lewis

WELCOME *to* THE DALLES

simply sunsational!

TOP 10 TRUE WESTERN TOWNS OF THE YEAR 2014

BALDWIN SALOON

THE DALLES AREA CHAMBER OF COMMERCE

541.296.2231
www.thedalleschamber.com

Mikayla Lewis caught her first walleye while fishing with guide Ed Iman near Rufus. Photo by Gary Lewis

jigs, Buzz Bombs, I guessed, by the way they dropped the blades down then ripped them up.

Eng decreed we would troll K15 and K16 Kwikfish, wrapped with sardine fillets.

Some days the trolling works better, sometimes the hover fishing works best, some days jigs are what they want.

We trolled from downriver up past the mouth of the White Salmon then reeled in and drove downstream to start again.

Around us, the egg fishermen battled salmon and netted them. We watched the jig fishermen land a couple.

Just when we thought we should rig up with eggs, Cindy's rod bent over hard. When she turned to set the hook, the fish was gone. That kept us going for another hour.

Around us, fishermen battled bright kings and coho. We began to rig for bait. Eng and I set up rods and tied leaders. I had just knotted a leader to a swivel when my rod buried. I dropped the leader on the deck and grabbed the rod from the holder.

The fish shook his head with violent shakes and made several short runs. On the reel, the line counter read 68 and then I gained a little. Closer to the surface the fish peeled line like a freight train going away, and I couldn't stop it till the counter read 145. A sturgeon? When he turned, I battled him back to the boat. When the line counter read 13, I saw him flash. A king, fresh from the salt.

Now, almost at my feet, the fish dove for cover beneath the boat. The rod tip followed it down toward the kicker motor, the line was inches from the spinning prop.

Yanked out of my grip, the rod reversed and the tip plunged beneath the water.

In that moment, I knew two things with certainty. I should have put Rod Wrap on this handle and I'd better not drop a rod in front of Dave Eng, who knows more people than I do.

Time stood still. Eng turned his head. He didn't want to see it happen.

When the rod swiveled, the pistol grip rotated on my right pinky finger and my left hand clamped around the fore grip. I shoved the rod down while the fish dove. Moments later the fish was back to the boat and Eng scooped it up – 15 angry pounds of Columbia River salmon.

In the big river, an angler in a boat has a definite advantage. Downstream, where anglers anchor in 12 to 20 feet of water, spinners are a favored bait, but upstream, where salmon stack at mouths of rivers like the White Salmon, the Klickitat, the Wind and the Deschutes, hover-fishing, trolling and jigging are the tactics in play.

Trollers start downriver and motor up to pull the wiggling lures behind the boat. Hover-fishermen like to drift downstream while they watch the graph and keep their leads and eggs two cranks off the bottom. Jig fishermen prefer to start at the top of the hole and drift down, tempting salmon with bright painted lead and steel.

Salmon roll between the boats. Jet sleds and ski boats that do double duty as fishing craft drift this way and that. Fishermen wave and nod as they pass or curse when someone gets too close. They try to stay out of each other's way, but bright gashes in some of the boats speak to the accidents that happen out there in the chaos that is salmon season on the Columbia.

Chinook, silver, and sockeye salmon migrate through this section of the river on their way to their native streams.

In general, salmon spawn in late summer and fall and hatch in the spring. Species differ in timing of the runs but may share the same river for weeks leading up to the spawn.

Proper gear and bait selection, water reading skill, presentation, and strength are all required to subdue a salmon.

Chinook average 15 pounds but 20- and 30-pound fish are common. And every year a few lucky fishermen boat 40- and 50-pound fish. But chinook salmon do grow bigger.

Salmon may be found in eight to 45 feet of water with the bulk of the fish holding in ten to 16 feet close to shore.

One bet is to back-troll salmon plugs such as the Worden's Flatfish or Luhr-Jensen's Kwikfish. This

A great smallmouth taken in deep water. The predatory bass move in packs and often stage to target down-migrating fry. Plastics and deep-running crankbaits are good medicine for big smallmouth. Photo by Gary Lewis

technique works well on holding fish. Back the boat downstream while bouncing your lead and plug rig through fish-holding water. Lift the rod, and give line as needed to keep the lead bouncing and the lure working back to waiting fish. Set the hook when the line goes limp or breaks from the flow of the current.

When back-trolling, tie the line directly to the eye snap for best action. Also, use lighter line if you want the lure to dive deeper. Heavy line creates more drag, preventing the lure from diving as deep. The technique is effective because the lure backs fish down with the lure, daring them to strike or get out of the way.

One of the best techniques is hover-fishing. The angler ties up a rig that utilizes a 2-ounce weight to the swivel and a 30-inch leader with a 2/0 hook and a thumb-sized clump of salmon or steelhead eggs.

Drop the rig down, let the 2-ounce weight bounce then crank it up two turns. The bait, sometimes enhanced with a little Mack's Lure Smile Blade, runs at an angle. Salmon either move out of the way or mouth the bait. At first, the bite is hard to discern. All at once there is a heaviness in the rod tip. Set the hook hard. If you feel a 'bite' what you're probably feeling is the fish spitting the bait out.

Walleye

The first two weeks of April give anglers a chance at catching pre-spawn walleyes in the Columbia. The water is beginning to warm and the fish are healthy. Serious fishermen start fishing in early spring for the best chance at landing a big female, full of eggs. After the walleye spawn in May, good fishing will continue through October.

Walleye average four to eight pounds in the Columbia. They feed heavily on perch, northern pikeminnow (squawfish), bass, and shad. The biggest fish are females.

Walleye prefer a stone, gravel, or sandy bottom. For the best walleye water look for a section of river with shallow spawning runs, located close to deep pools or channels. Watch for places where small fry might congregate, and do your walleye hunting there. Jetties where riprap can hold minnows, drop-offs, ledges, rocky points, and gravel bars are some examples.

One effective rig that will take walleye throughout the season employs a three-foot leader, a light spinner blade, fluorescent green beads, and double hook setup

Steelhead can be taken on flies in the Columbia.
Photo by Paul Anderson, Fly Fishing Strategies

creatures, shad strain their food through gill-rakers. Running upriver, they strike mainly out of frustration, instead of feeding impulses. Small spoons, spinners, and yarn flies will bring fish to the net, but jigs are used far more than any other tackle.

Rig a sliding sinker on the main line to a barrel swivel and 30 inches of leader to the jig. Plain lead jigs with no color will catch fish. When the bite slows, add a little color.

Timing the shad run is the most important thing. When 10,000 fish a day are going over Bonneville Dam, throw the tackle in the car and head for the water.

Make money with Northern Pikeminnow

In the Columbia, they congregate near dams, islands, jetties, river mouths, riprap, and rocky ledges. Their principal foods are salmon and steelhead smolts, crayfish, baby lamprey eels, and freshwater clams. Since salmon and steelhead smolts are disoriented after coming through dams, pikeminnow make short work of them. Northern pikeminnow have thrived in the slower water of the Columbia River since the dams were introduced. Salmon and steelhead have been the losers.

For this reason, northern pikeminnow should not be returned to the water alive. They make good food for sturgeon and

baited with a whole nightcrawler. The nightcrawler is rigged to hang straight down on the two hooks. Five inches of hollow core lead on a slider rig keeps the bait bouncing along the bottom.

Baits should be presented on a long line or off to the side of the boat's path of travel. When you feel the strike, drop the rod and count to three before lifting the tip, gently setting the hook.

Smallmouth Bass

Smallmouth bass prefer warmer, flowing water and can be found in great numbers around weed beds, grassy banks, along the seams of riffles, deep along rock walls, and in gravel flats. On clear summer days when the sun is high, the biggest fish will be found in deeper water. On overcast days or when the sun is low on the horizon, smallmouth can be caught on or closer to the surface.

They are aggressive predators, feeding on smaller fish, insects, leeches, snails, and crayfish. Since big bass eat little bass, the smaller bass tend to stay in schools away from larger fish. If you are catching little bass, move to deeper water to target larger fish.

Crankbaits and minnow imitations work very well in smallmouth water, especially along ledges or around submerged

structure. Use patterns to imitate local baitfish. Chub, perch and rainbow patterns work well for minnow imitations. Orange and olive crayfish patterns are good crankbait options.

Another good tactic is to dead-drift a plastic worm, allowing it to tumble through the best bass-holding water. Rig the worm weedless (with hook point buried in the worm) to minimize hooking up on the bottom.

American Shad

Shad were introduced into Oregon in the mid-1880's. The spawning run begins when river waters warm in the spring. Mature adults average three to four pounds in size, and may return to the river to spawn as many as four times.

For shad, light gear is preferable. Six- to ten-pound test line and a slow-action rod makes a good combination for the angler who favors spinning or casting gear. Small jig heads baited with a small rubber grub are employed and allowed to hang in the current. Best colors include red, yellow, white, pink, blue, gold, and silver. Flash and color are important. Depth is crucial and enough weight should be used in fast water to take the lure close to the bottom.

Feeding on microscopic

Ed Iman, shad fishing below Bonneville. Photo by Gary Lewis

great fertilizer for flower gardens.

Most pikeminnow are caught downstream of dams in fast water from five to 30 feet deep. Many anglers fish at night to capitalize on the fish's tendency to move into the shallows in the dark.

Northern pikeminnow average twelve inches to twenty-four. Females make up the majority of the bigger fish and can reach weights of ten pounds.

Salmon and steelhead rods are good choices to use in the pursuit of pikeminnow. Ten or twelve-pound test line is adequate.

Though you can catch northern pikeminnow on a variety of gear, there are several methods that improve the odds.

One of the most effective techniques is fishing with plastic grubs and worms from 1-1/2 inches up to 6 inches long. When fishing during the day, the best colors are smoke and chartreuse, and white. But don't be afraid to try something different. When night fishing, red, purple, and black glitter are effective. Orange-brown imitates the crayfish and can also be a good pattern.

When using grubs, a jig head is most commonly employed. The best weights are 1/8 ounce up to ½ ounce. When using worms, a sliding sinker is sometimes used on the leader. In faster water, the worm is left unweighted and a sliding sinker is attached to the main line.

When fishing in ten to twenty feet of water, use enough weight to "tick" the bottom from time to time. This is fishing that is hard on tackle. Expect to lose gear when fishing for pikeminnow. If you're not tying new rigs often, you're probably not fishing where the fish are.

Cast across and upstream, allowing the lure to sink and bounce. Let it drift. Strikes can be triggered, on occasion, by imparting action of some kind. Slowing down or speeding up the retrieve can pay off.

Bait fishing is another way to catch pikeminnow. Worms, chicken liver, cluster salmon eggs, and strips of fish are good choices. Depending on the type of fishing you do, you will need weights ranging from split shot to ½ ounce. Tie a #2 or #4 hook to an eighteen to 24-inch section of leader. Tie a swivel to the leader and slide another swivel over the main line. Use a bead to protect the knot. Tie a four-inch section of line to the sliding swivel and attach a piece of hollow-core pencil lead. A bullet sinker, or bottom-walker rig can be used in place of the sliding swivel if desired. Plunking and drifting bait can work equally well for pikeminnow.

Spinners and spoons are also effective for pikeminnow. Again, it is important to use a lure that will sink fast enough in the swift water where these fish are found. Additional weight can be added in the form of split shot. ¼ ounce

This nice salmon was taken on a fly at the mouth of a tributary. It takes a specialized technique but when a big streamer runs through a school, it's likely to provoke a chaser. Photo by Paul Anderson, Fly Fishing Strategies

John Kruse picked up this small-mouth in the John Day pool.

and heavier spinners are favored by most. A variety of retrieves can pay off for pikeminnow. Experiment until you find a retrieve that works.

Wobbling spoons imitate baitfish. Pikeminnow will take them retrieved or jigged. The jig simulates a disoriented baitfish and can be particularly effective.

Trolled behind a boat, crankbaits are potent pikeminnow lures. The important thing about using crankbaits is matching the lure to the depth of the water. Use a crankbait that will dive almost to the bottom, fishing effectively in the fish-holding zone.

Walleye fishermen have to adjust their hooksets when targeting pikeminnow. This is a fish with a harder mouth. Set the hook fast when you feel the light tap that means a pikeminnow has struck.

The Bonneville Power Administration in cooperation with the Washington and Oregon Fish Management Agencies and Tribal Administrations sponsors a sport reward program designed to thin northern pikeminnow populations in the Columbia. The intent is to reduce the number of predators preying on steelhead and salmon. For the first 100 fish you catch in a season, you can earn $4.00 per fish. After that, the BPA will pay up to $8.00 depending upon how many fish you turn in. Tagged

fish rewards are worth $500 per tagged fish. Every Columbia River pikeminnow over nine inches long is worth money.

To learn more about season dates, how-to and where-to, and payment possibilities, call 800-858-9015 or visit the website at: www.pikeminnow.org.

Other Species

Largemouth bass, yellow perch and crappie can be found in the Columbia's slower water. Fish protected areas where the current is slowed. Target bass and crappie near piers, bridge abutments, rocky points and other structure. Several species of carp and catfish are available throughout the river.

A big sturgeon goes back in the water. Photo by Greg Gustafson, Sturgeon River Monsters

Boat Launches

In the area immediately below Bonneville Dam, there are three good launches on the Oregon side.

The Fishery is accessible from eastbound and westbound I-84. There are two ramps: the lower ramp is larger and most used. It has two launch lanes (best bet is to use the downriver lane on this ramp) and ample dock space. Four-wheel drive is recommended for upper ramp. It can be windy in this section of the river and strong currents are possible.

Dalton Point is accessible from eastbound I-84. There is one ramp with two lanes and no dock.

Rooster Rock is accessible from eastbound and westbound I-84. There is one ramp with four lanes and a small dock. This launch is wheelchair accessible and is sheltered from wind and currents.

But don't use this ramp when the river is low.

Above the dam, there is a marina at Cascade Locks Marine Park. Good launches are available at Hood River, Mayer State Park and The Dalles.

Be Careful

The Columbia River has been tamed, turned into a highway for heavy commercial traffic. It is controlled by dams, used to generate electricity, and provide food. It is also a playground for water skiers, hunters, fishermen and pleasure boaters. But beneath its benign exterior beats the heart of a beast. This river can kill you. Deep, strong currents called undertows can pull you down and keep you down. High winds can whip up whitecaps that can swamp a small boat or beat your craft to pieces on a jetty. Sandbars that can destroy your outboard prop lurk beneath the surface in the middle of the river. Drifting debris can eviscerate your boat or destroy your motor. And a tugboat pushing a barge can crush your boat beneath its prow. Those are just a few of the ways that the river can kill. Don't help it by operating a boat under the influence of alcohol.

Learn where the navigable channel is so you don't run aground in shallow water. Learn to recognize navigational aids such as red and green buoys, range markers and the five-blast danger signal from a vessel bearing down on you. See the Oregon Boater's Handbook for more information.

Setting anchor and pulling anchor are operations fraught with danger in a river as powerful and prone to change as is the Columbia. Old pilings, submerged cars, floating timber, old fishnets and many other hazards lurk beneath the surface. Commercial traffic, changing tides and varying water levels are all factors you must deal with, each time you boat on the Columbia. When at anchor, be on the lookout for floating debris that may come down on the anchor line.

The mouth of the White Salmon as seen from the slopes above downtown Hood River. Photo by Gary Lewis

Badger Creek

Length..................................... 25 miles

Regulations .... Artificial fly & lure

Trail .... Easy gradient

Elevation at source .... 4,400 feet

Species: Rainbow, brook trout

Best Methods: Fly fishing

Tips: Check streamside boulders and rocks for insects and try to match the hatch

Leave your bait box at home and bring your fly tackle.

It took us an hour longer to find the trailhead than it should have, especially since I had been there before. But find it we did and we parked the truck and Jennifer and I hoisted our packs and headed west into the sunset, on foot along a trail along a creek named for a flesh-eating mammal that burrows in the ground.

Badger Creek, a tributary of Tygh Creek in the White River drainage, flows out of Badger Lake on the southeast side of Mt. Hood. One of the best places to start is at the end of the road. A small parking area at the trailhead is the jumping off point that leads up into the Badger Creek Wilderness.

We carried fly rods and a box of dry flies. If we couldn't catch trout on top we wouldn't catch them at all.

An hour before dark we found a campsite. Jen set up her tent and I stripped cedar boughs and laid my sleeping bag beneath the open sky.

In the morning we ate a light breakfast then rigged our fly rods. I would use a No. 14 Parachute Adams, while Jennifer would fish a Purple Haze which is essentially the same fly except it is tied in purple.

We walked back down the trail to where the path split from the creek and waded in our hiking boots to the bottom of the first run.

While we were still close to the path we caught small fish, the farther upstream we went, as the cliffs closed in on both sides, the trout were bigger. In one run, a ten-inch rainbow turned for Jen's dry, but escaped without feeling the steel.

We took turns fishing each run, each trout a gift, a jewel. One was a brook trout, a small one, the rest were rainbows, spotted, brilliant, wild.

After clawing our way through the vine maple we looked into a long, classic pool, crystal clear and

A good trail leads up Badger Creek to fast dry fly action. Photo by Gary Lewis

stood in the water to cast upstream. After Jen caught a little one, I made 15 casts and had 15 takes in a row. One trout was clearly bigger than the rest and it took my fly at least four times. Each time I missed it. Finally it rejected the Adams and it was Jennifer's turn. Another grab and then another and she caught the nine-inch trophy.

After two hours we were close to camp again and a pool that should have contained a good fish only produced little ones.

In Badger's riffled water, use small attractor flies like the Purple Haze, Parachute Adams, Humpy, Royal Wulff, and Irresistible. In longer, slower runs, switch to soft-hackle wet flies. Fish beadhead nymphs beneath a strike indicator in deeper sections.

Here the trout average about six inches and can run to 15 inches. In most runs, a nine-incher is considered the trophy. Most of the angling pressure focuses on the first half-mile of creek upstream from the parking area on the lower reach. Upstream, there is some pressure down from Badger Lake. For bigger fish, walk for a mile or two before wading in. Bring mosquito repellent and watch out for rattlesnakes.

There are primitive campgrounds at Badger Lake and at Bonney Crossing

Directions

Roads cross the stream at Bonney Crossing and just below Badger Lake. Downstream, the creek is crossed by several smaller roads and Forest Road 47 and again at Tygh Valley, by Highway 197.

Para Wulff Purple
Courtesy Fly & Field Outfitters

We have seen it called the Purple Haze, the Purple Parachute Adams and this one is called the Para Wulff Purple. Whatever you call it, wherever you fish it, chances are, it will become one of your favorite dry flies, a pattern to turn to when the fish are eating mayflies on the surface.

The parachute configuration lends to its castability. It drops to the water softly and the twin wingposts help to track it in riffled water. Fish this one in a size 12 to imitate a March Brown or tie on a size 18 when blue-winged olives are on the surface.

Start with a No. 12-18 dry fly hook. Tie the tail with deer hair. Build the body with purple dubbing and rib with Flashabou. Tie a double wingpost of white calftail. Finish with a brown and a grizzly hackle wrapped parachute style.

Resources

Nearest cities/towns:
Wamic

Accommodations:
River Run Lodge, Imperial River Company, Oasis Resort

Camping:
Primitive, Badger Lake Campground

Tackle:
Deschutes Canyon Fly Shop
www.flyfishingdeschutes.com
Deschutes Angler Fly Shop
www.deschutesangler.com

Visitor information:
Mt. Hood Area Chamber
www.mthood.org
503-622-3017

Badger Creek rainbows are not all that big, but they're fun to catch on tiny attractors. Photo by Gary Lewis

This nine inch rainbow was the morning's biggest trophy. Photo by Gary Lewis

Badger Lake

Size .... 40 acres at full pool

Maximum Depth .... 40 feet

Trail .... Fisherman's trail around the lake

Elevation .... 4,472 feet

Best Fly Patterns:
Dry .... #14 parachute adams
#10 flying ant
Wet .... #14 callibaetis nymph
#10 Woolly Bugger

Best Lures:
Trolling ....F4 Flatfish in frog, perch or black
Casting .... 1/4 oz. Kastmaster spoon
1/4 oz. Kamlooper spoon

Species: Stocked rainbow, brook trout

Best Methods: Fly fishing or trolling

Tips: Car top or inflatable boats only. Road No. 140 is closed to trailers of any kind due to a steep, narrow grade, lack of pullouts, and very rough road bed.

Iral Harmon of Fisherman's Marine and Outdoor is a regular visitor to Badger Lake. Here he trolls his way to a quick limit. Photo by Robert Campbell.

Do not let rumors of the rough, dangerous road deter you from visiting Badger Lake, as I did for years. Yes, the road in is bad, but if you have a reliable four-wheel-drive vehicle and drive slowly and carefully, Badger is a great lake to visit.

If you are fortunate to be a passenger on the drive instead of the white-knuckled driver, the trip is actually really cool. This part of the Mt. Hood Forest is beautiful, and once you get up top, the woods are a wonderful mix of grand fir, mountain hemlock, silver fir, Engelmann spruce and vine maple. Wildlife abounds, including deer, elk, a wide variety of birds, bear, marten, pika, squirrels, cougar, and yes, badger. A friend who hunts turkey says the area is flush with them. The lake itself is teeming with trout, including wild and planted rainbows, and brook trout.

Badger was a natural lake that was dammed at the outlet to increase its size and storage capacity for irrigation purposes downstream. Aside from the earthen dam on the north end, it has all the appearances and characteristics of a natural lake. However, once drawdown occurs during mid-to late summer, its irrigation purpose becomes obvious, as luxuriant littoral zones turn to mud flats and exposed stumps. Visit Badger Lake as soon as the roads are clear—usually late June or early July—and this is one of the most beautiful lakes in the Mt. Hood National Forest. The lake is also the source of Badger Creek, a pretty little mountain stream that provides excellent dry fly fishing for wild rainbow.

Besides its gorgeous setting in a glacially-carved cirque, another great reason to venture to Badger Lake is its trout. The lake is stuffed with them. Early in the season the trout are scattered and you can catch them virtually anywhere on the lake. Badger has its own unique strain of rainbow trout that has been isolated for millennia due to a falls on the lower creek. This native strain of rainbow is wild and pure, and one of the most beautiful types of trout I have ever seen. The wild trout are easy to discern from the planted variety, as they tend to be smaller and are much more colorful. The larger of these wild trout, say 9-inches or above, have the wonderful trait of having a splash of reddish-orange on the tips of their dorsal fins. They also have distinct parr marks. If God were to ask James Prosek to paint him a gorgeous trout, the noted author might very well serve up a rendition of a Badger Lake redband.

When I visit Badger, I choose to release any of these wild redband trout due to their uniqueness. Picture fish, I call them, for that is their best purpose: a quick photo followed by a quick release. Badger Lake is also full of stocked rainbow and brook trout, and unfortunately for them, these two varieties are the victims of my profiling, especially the brook trout. Brook trout are actually a char and were introduced to Oregon from the East Coast sometime in the early 1900s. As an introduced species, it makes more sense to me to harvest them rather than a native rainbow. They are delicious. Of course, the hatchery trout are there to serve one of three purposes for anglers: breakfast, lunch or dinner.

Though Badger is located in a steep-sided bowl at the head of Badger Creek Canyon, it is blessed with abundant shallows and productive shorelines. Roughly 1/3 of the lake qualifies as shoal area, and it is these shallow areas that provide massive amounts of food for the fish in the form of abundant aquatic insect populations. This makes Badger an incredibly productive lake for the fly angler. Kicking along the shore in a pontoon boat or float tube and firing ant patterns at the shoreline shallows around stumps and under overhanging brush is fun casting and productive fishing.

From mid-summer on, Badger has incredible midge hatches condensed into the morning and evening hours. When these bugs are coming off, a chironomid pupa fished under an indicator is hard to beat. Size 14 or smaller in black, grey or red are standard here. The trout in Badger are also eager risers to dry flies, so don't hesitate to throw an adult midge or Griffith's gnat during midge hatches. You will catch trout from 4-inches long to several pounds out of Badger, though fish of greater than 16-inches are rare.

Callibaetis mayfly hatches can also be profuse at Badger Lake, especially if you are there on a cloudy or drizzly day in the summer. There seems to be two generations of this bug at Badger, a No.14 in mid-summer, then a smaller No. 16-18 insect in the fall. Match the size for best results. The hatch timing varies with the weather, but expect activity on almost a daily basis anywhere from 10:00 a.m. to 3:00 p.m. Also, this is one of the few places I have fished where the trout absolutely feast on Callibaetis spinner falls, rather than casually slurping them once in awhile. Watch for these mating swarms in the afternoon hours at the edges of the lake, especially along brushy banks near the dam.

I once spent several hours fishing a mayfly spinner fall at Badger while sitting in my Caddis float tube at the edge of the lake, my butt resting on the bottom in inches of water. The trout were in the shallows, cruising for

Resources

Nearest cities/towns:
Wamic

Accommodations:
River Run Lodge, Imperial River Company, Oasis Resort

Camping:
Primitive, Badger Lake Campground

Tackle:
Deschutes Canyon Fly Shop
www.flyfishingdeschutes.com
Deschutes Angler Fly Shop
www.deschutesangler.com

Visitor information:
Mt. Hood Area Chamber, www.mthood.org
503-622-3017

Wild redband trout are present in Badger Lake and at times are very willing to take dry flies. Photo by Robert Campbell.

spent spinners and jumping clear of the water to take mayflies out of the air! Even though the only spinner pattern I had with me was a black henwing two sizes too big, I still caught lots of trout sight-fishing to cruisers, and most of them were pulled from water less than a foot deep! This was some of the most enjoyable fly fishing I have ever experienced, anywhere.

Of course, the venerable woolly bugger in black or brown is a killer pattern here, especially in the morning and evening. Brown is my favorite, as there are plentiful crawdads here. A Callibaetis nymph fished on a clear intermediate line with a long, fine leader will also take Badger Lake trout on any day, especially if you can stand to use a painfully slow hand twist retrieve to accurately imitate the natural. Mercer's Poxyback Cahill is a killer pattern here and at many other lakes where I've tried it.

There doesn't necessarily need to be ants on the water at Badger to justify using an ant pattern. I once fished Badger sometime after an ant flight had occurred, but there were none visible on the water. However, the trout remembered, and I caught and released a couple dozen brook trout casting a No. 10 flying ant pattern to the brushy northeast shoreline near the dam.

Gear fishermen will do well casting a variety of lures here including Acme spoons like the Little Cleo, Wob-L-Rite, Kamlooper and Kastmaster. Spinners like the Blue Fox, Worden's Rooster Tail, Panther Martin and Mepps are also productive. But if you really want to have productive lure fishing at Badger, it is hard to beat trolling a small Flatfish, Hot Shot or Frisky Fly behind a small lake troll or tandem Indiana spinner rig. The key is to troll slowly, and you will be utterly amazed how many fish are in this lake as you troll parallel to the shoreline in 6-20 feet of water.

Bait fishing is legal at Badger at the time of this writing, however, I don't recommend it as it is difficult to release a fish deeply hooked with bait with any reasonable expectation of survival. Remember those native redbands, and do your part to conserve them for future generations.

There is a nice campground located on the creek just below the lake, and a few unimproved sites on the lake that would require no trace camping techniques. Always check with the Forest Service for road conditions before venturing into Badger.

Directions:

The traditional route from Portland is to take Highway 26 east. Three miles past Government Camp, take the Highway 35 exit and follow it approximately 7 miles to Bennett Pass. Take Forest Road No. 3550 approximately 4 miles toward Camp Windy. Turn east on Forest Road No. 4860, then left (north) onto Road No. 140 for the final descent into the lake.

A slightly better route, in my opinion, is as follows: Head east from Government Camp and take Highway 35 exit, but turn off on road No. 48 just after crossing the White River. Follow this to the Forest Road No. 4860 cut-off, and then follow this north all the way to Road No. 140 for the final descent into the lake. While longer in miles, this route seems slightly smoother and safer.

Casting ant patterns to shoreline structure is a great way to take brook trout at Badger Lake during the summer months, sometimes from mere inches of water! Photo by Robert Campbell.

Mt. Hood as seen from the southwest. Photo by Robert Campbell

Boulder Lake

Size ....20 acres

Depth............................Deepest against slide

Trail .... .5 miles

Difficulty...Easy climb

Elevation:
  Trailhead.. 4,363 feet
  Lake.. 4,539 feet

GPS Coordinates:
  Trailhead............N 45 15.556, W 121 33.561
  Lake....................N 45 15.479, W 121 34.018

Species: Brook trout

Best Methods: Fly and casting bubble

Tips:
Plan to wade out in the shallows to reach feeding fish

A look at a map shows several approaches to the trailhead. From State Highway 35, the road skirts Bennett Pass. Another route leads in from Wamic and Rock Creek Reservoir. A nice paved road leads away from Highway 26 down into the White River canyon then up through stands of tall firs and clearings colonized by reprod.

A wrong turn can put you close to the lake but miles from the trailhead. Watch for blacktail deer and elk on the side of canyon and forest grouse on the roadside.

Boulder Creek splashes down and runs through a culvert at the trailhead. Your first clue as to the temperament of the lake is the temperature of the creek. In June, the water runs warm because the lake is shallow around most of its circumference.

The trail leads up and away from the road. In two minutes, the road is out of view and soon the shade of the trees strips away the heat of a summer day. On the first bench, a quarter mile from the trailhead, the hiker reaches Spinning Lake, a one-acre still water in a grove of silvered firs.

It seems like it is only a few steps and then Boulder Lake is glimpsed through the timber. Several primitive campsites are scattered along the shore. The lake is light green shading to dark in the center.

On the south bank, talus slides create structure and habitat for trout. On the north shore, a narrow sandy beach gives way to clear water and a muddy, sandy bottom that is nice to wade sans hiking boots. Fallen timber creates shadows on the bottom, shadows that harbor speckled char - brook trout - on the prowl for their next meal.

Like most backcountry waters, the trout are stocked as fingerlings, every other year. Here, the brookies don't realize their potential in the length department. In fact, the first fish caught was an

Hundreds of backcountry lakes in the Cascades offer good fishing and solitude for those willing to hike a few miles away from the road. Photo by Gary Lewis

Jennifer Lewis admires a brook trout from Boulder Lake. Photo by Gary Lewis

older trout with a head that looked like it was transplanted from a much larger fish. Food can be scarce in some alpine lakes.

When we fished it, the lake produced trout that averaged 6 to 8 inches. It was June and the spent hulls of mayflies could be seen on the driftwood, but clouds of midges buzzed over the surface and a chocolate caddis, about a No. 12, struggled up out of the surface film. We caught a few on fly rods then switched to spinning setups with casting bubbles followed by a fly (or two) on fluorocarbon leaders.

As the sun dropped behind the ridge line, the fishing improved and so did our appetites. Camp smokes began to puff up through the trees from two camps on the shore. Each of us had battled numerous fish and we kept a few for the fire.

Directions

From Highway 26, take Forest Road 43, headed northeast. Cross the White River and make a right turn onto Forest Road 48, headed east. After crossing Boulder Creek, look for a sharp left turn and the sign to Boulder Lake.

A Boulder Lake brookie taken on a long cast and small wet fly.

Black Flying Ant
Tied by Gary Lewis

When you're fishing mountain lakes for trout or prospecting a pond for bluegill, keep your eye open for ants. On windy days, the bugs are blown out of trees and shoreside grass to waiting fish.

You should be watching for flying ants, because you can bet the fish are. If fish are rising along the shore and no apparent hatch is in evidence, tie on an ant pattern and move your boat or float tube within range. Let it drift or impart a little action as if its wings are fluttering.

Resources

Nearest cities/towns:
Government Camp

Tackle:
Top Stop Food & Fuel

The Fly Fishing Shop, Welches
www.flyfishusa.com

Visitor information:
Mt. Hood Area Chamber, www.mthood.org
503-622-3017

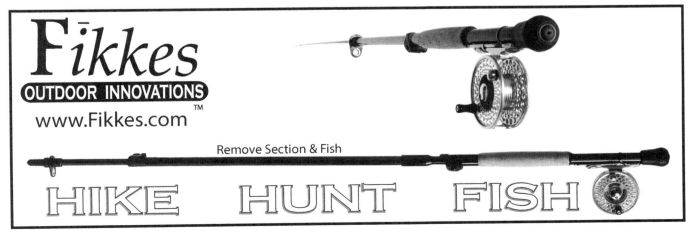

Clear Lake

Size ....Just under 500 acres at full pool

Maximum Depth............................... 22 feet

Difficulty .... Easy

Elevation .... 3,518 feet

Species: Stocked rainbow, brook trout

Best Methods: Bait, lure or fly. When the fish are on, it all works.

Tips: A brown Woolly Bugger is hard to beat at Clear Lake.

Clear lake is a mountain reservoir created in 1959 with the damming of Clear Creek by Wasco Dam. The quality of the trout fishing is very much affected by snowpack and subsequent water levels in the reservoir. When at full pool, Clear Lake looks very much like a natural body of water. But during a period of low snowpack and hot, dry summers where irrigation demands are substantial, Clear Lake is rapidly drawn down to expose the multitude of stumps that were left as the forest was cleared to make way for the lake.

During some years the lake is drained to the point that only a small puddle remains in the former creek bed, which is surrounded by acres of reddish, knee-deep muck. Despite these fluctuations in water level, Clear Lake still provides some good trout fishing for stocked rainbow trout and "wild" brook trout. String together a couple of high snowpack years and cooler summers, and the fishing at Clear Lake can be phenomenal.

Clear Lake is not a particularly deep reservoir, and when water levels are stable there is abundant weed and phytoplankton growth that support an excellent food base for the trout. When things are good, the trout grow quickly. After Timothy Lake, Clear Lake is probably the next best place in the Mt. Hood Forest to catch big trout. There are plentiful brook trout here that average a plump 10-14 inches, and much bigger specimens up to five pounds are available. Also like Timothy, the brook trout here are suckers for crawdad fly patterns, and a brown Woolly Bugger stripped or trolled on a clear intermediate line is deadly at Clear Lake.

If brook trout are your intended target, then focus your attention on the remnant stumps and logs that dot the shallow areas of the lake. Cast your fly or lure as close to this cover as possible and hold on. Yes, you will lose some gear fishing in this manner, but you will also catch more trout. When brook trout aren't actively foraging, they lurk around woody debris, and this is where you will consistently catch

Clear Lake is an underutilized resource that sometimes provides excellent trout fishing for rainbow and brook trout. Photo by Robert Campbell.

them. I know one stump in the north arm of the lake that has provided a large brook trout EVERY time I have fished it over the past ten years!

Here is the program: the stump is located in about five feet of water not far from shore. I quietly approach in my boat or pontoon to within casting range, then cast a #8 brown woolly bugger to within a couple feet of the stump and just beyond it. I then countdown seven seconds while the fly sinks, then retrieve the fly past the log in short, quick strips. The retrieve never lasts very long! Good luck finding your own "Magic Stump" at Clear Lake!

The rainbow trout fishing at Clear Lake can also be exceptional at times. The Oregon Department of Fish and Wildlife delivers a steady supply of 8-12 inch rainbows to Clear Lake, and if conditions are right the trout grow rapidly. It is not uncommon for these "planters" to reach a chunky 14-plus inches by the end of a productive summer. Furthermore, if water levels remain fairly stable along with the food supply, then wintertime survival of the trout is good and you can expect some excellent fishing for larger hold-over trout the following spring. That's how it went in the Spring/Summer of 2004 when I got a phone call from a co-worker at Fisherman's Marine and Outdoor, Tom Thorud.

Tom is somewhat well-known in the Pacific Northwest as a walleye fisherman who pioneered effective techniques on the Columbia and Willamette Rivers for that introduced species. But what fewer people know is that Tom is also an extremely accomplished salmon, trout and steelhead angler. In mid-May of 2004, I received the call from an excited Thorud who said, "Robert, you just have to get up to Clear Lake with your fly rod, it's absolutely loaded with big trout this year!"

Now I could tell by the excitement in Tom's voice that he wasn't pulling my leg, so I did just as advised. Tom was right. That year the lake was full of aggressive hold-over rainbows averaging 16-22 inches and weighing from 2-4 pounds. These fished seemed to prefer the deeper water of the main lake around the old creek bed, and all you had to do was slow-troll a Woolly Bugger about 12-feet down in 20-feet of water and you were in them. The strikes were savage, and we started fishing 8-pound SeaGuar fluorocarbon leaders to keep from snapping them off. Because these trout had been feasting on natural forage, their meat was firm and bright pinkish-orange— they were delicious! Of course we caught-and-released far more than we took home for dinner.

ODFW also stocks Clear Lake several times a year with much larger "trophy trout" that more resemble the larger hold-over fish. From time to time they also raid their stock of brood trout at Oak Springs Hatchery on the Deschutes River and put some truly monster-sized trout into Clear. If you have ever stopped at the hatchery and viewed the trout in these pens then I know that I now have your attention! The brood fish that they use for hatchery production are immense. These trout run from about six-pounds on up to the high-teens in weight. There are a few swimming around in there that might push twenty pounds! And it's possible that at some point many of these trout could end up in Clear

Resources

Nearest cities/towns:
Government Camp

Camping:
Clear Lake Campground

Tackle:
The Fly Fishing Shop, Welches
www.flyfishusa.com

Top Stop Food & Fuel

Visitor information:
Mt. Hood Area Chamber
www.mthood.org
503-622-3017

From this photo it is easy to see why easterners often refer to brook trout as "square tails." Photo by Robert Campbell.

Lake. I caught one of these once from my "Magic Stump" in the north arm of the lake. The fish was 27-inches long, looked to be about 8 lbs, and I released it to get even bigger. Talk about a battle on a six-weight!

Early in the season when full, Clear Lake is blessed with extensive shoal area, which means that you can troll just about anywhere on the lake and expect to find some fish. Once draw-down commences and the lake begins to shrink, the trout often congregate in the old creek channels and it's possible to have some really great fishing if a big concentration of fish is located. For brook trout I prefer the stump fields in the north and west arms, though you may catch them anywhere on the lake. There are a few areas where they congregate in shallow water in the fall to spawn, but these fish should be left alone to do their thing and provide for the future of the fishery. Spawning brook trout have mushy, tasteless flesh, so they are worthless on the table anyway.

Be advised that Clear Lake is also famous for its reliable afternoon winds, though it may blow here at any time. Float tube anglers and pontooners beware, the wind can be so strong here that it will quickly bully you across the lake, and it's a long walk back around. If the wind becomes too much to deal with at Clear Lake, I usually put to shore and fish from the bank. There are plentiful areas around the lake to easily bank fish, especially if draw-down has occurred. That's one thing that I like about Clear Lake, it is easy to wade fish from shore as there are lots of areas where you will have

clearance for your back cast.

In the fall of 2013, I finished up my trout fishing for the year with an excellent dry fly session on the west arm of Clear Lake. Dusk was approaching quickly and there was that certain chill on the water. I could see my breath in the air for the first time in months. I had just loaded my pontoon boat and most of my equipment when the midges started hatching. It took awhile for the adults to get off the water, and the trout were exploding on #16 midges on the surface. Best of all, this action was taking place within 20-30 feet of the shore. For once I had the right fly on me, and I caught-and-released many plump rainbows and brookies in the fading light as Bob Dylan blew his harp over the truck stereo. Better yet, there was not another living soul around. An evening like that stays with you and provides solace in January when all of the steelhead streams are blown-out.

At this time there seems to be a robust population of brook trout in Clear Lake, and they are easier to catch here than their selective counterparts at Timothy. Anglers of all types and skill levels will enjoy fishing at Clear Lake, for quality trout can be taken on any technique or type of gear. Bait fishing from shore is easy and productive for most of the season.

Rainbow trout grow quickly in Clear Lake during high water years when weed growth and food are abundant. Photo by Robert Campbell.

A lenticular cloud begins to form over the summit of Mt. Hood as the wind pushes moisture-laden air upslope. Photo by Robert Campbell.

Trollers will catch plenty of nice fish on small plugs, wobblers and spinners. Fly anglers will delight in plentiful midge and Callibaetis mayfly hatches. And don't forget the crawdads. Brook trout everywhere find it hard to resist a small crawdad, and that's why the brown Woolly Bugger is so effective at Clear Lake and many other lakes in the Mt. Hood Forest.

Not a fly fisherman? You can still effectively fish flies on light spinning gear by employing a clear torpedo float like my accomplished co-author, Gary Lewis, so often does. It is also easy and effective to troll a Woolly Bugger on spinning gear by adding just enough weight in front of it to keep it down. Experiment with different weights and trolling speeds until the trout tell you what the right combination is by bending your rod!

There is a nice forest campground on the east side of the lake located in a grove of mountain hemlock and Pacific silver fir. Large rhododendrons are plentiful here and the blooms are beautiful in late June. The campground has 22 total mixed sites (tent or RV), and five sites just for tent campers. Due to the elevation and heavy snowfall in the area, the campground is open seasonally at this time from June 15th to September 30th. Because of the continuous plowing of Highway 26, the access road to Clear Lake, road #2630, is often blocked by a large snow bank after most of the snow at pass level has melted off. Check with Zig Zag Ranger Station for road conditions and access early in the season (503-622-3191.)

Directions

Follow Highway 26 east from Government Camp approximately 9 miles and take Road #2630 south for one mile to the campground and boat ramp. There is a sign for this exit. Just before the campground, a rough road forks to the right, which winds its way around the lake before ending at the west arm. Note: At low water levels, the boat ramp here is only usable by small craft.

Frog Lake

Size	11 acres
Depth	6 feet
Difficulty	Easy
Elevation	3,800 feet

Species: Rainbow, cutthroat, brook trout

Best Methods: Fly, still-fishing

Tips: Bring a float tube or a raft

Surrounded by firs and hemlocks, Frog Lake is an 11-acre body of water high in the White River watershed. Very close to the highway and stocked with rainbow trout, the lake is popular with traveling anglers and is a good place to bring children or beginners. Hatchery rainbows average between 8 and 11 inches, though bigger fish are present. ODFW also stocks surplus brood stock in Frog Lake.

The bank is fishable, but fly fishermen will do best from a float tube or a small boat. Motors are not allowed.

All methods work well at Frog Lake, but fly-fishing can be very productive. One effective technique incorporates the spinning rod, a casting bubble and flies.

The casting bubble is the key to making this technique effective. It must be the type that can be filled with water, which provides the weight necessary for long-distance casting. Whether fishing on the surface or below the surface, the best choice is the medium size, clear plastic bubble that is the approximate size of a chicken egg.

Slide the bubble over your main line and tie on a No. 12 or 14 black barrel swivel. Knot a three-foot, four-pound test leader to your barrel swivel, then tie on the fly. For starters, use a wet fly such as a No. 8 Woolly Bugger, or No. 10 Woolly Worm. Good nymph patterns are flies like the beadhead Pheasant Tail, or Prince Nymph. When fishing for bigger fish, try minnow patterns.

Cast, tighten up the line, and begin to reel – slowly. Vary the depth and retrieve until you find the fish. A slow retrieve is usually the most effective.

Spoons that imitate baitfish work well at Frog Lake. Little Cleos, Triple Teasers, and Kastmasters are some of the more popular models. Smaller is better when targeting hatchery trout. Add a snap swivel, then tie the spoon directly to your main line and add a little weight if needed. Cast, let it sink, and

This unidentified angler was witnessed beautifully casting some tight loops while trout fishing at Frog Lake. Photo by Robert Campbell.

retrieve just fast enough to keep your lure wobbling, not spinning.

The best plugs for catching these trout are minnow imitations. Try small Rapalas and Flatfish. You may need to add a little weight for casting. Vary your retrieve and depth until you start hooking rainbows.

The Frog Lake Campground opens in June each year. 33 basic sites provide tables, cooking grills, toilets and drinking water.

Directions

The road to Frog Lake can be found less than 8 miles southeast of Government Camp on Highway 26. Watch for the sign at Forest Road 2610. The lake is a short drive east of the highway.

Mt. Hood provides a scenic background while angling at Frog Lake.
Photo by Gary Lewis

T-Tag Woolly Bugger
Tied by Gary Lewis

You know that annoying piece of plastic that hangs the tag on a new shirt? It's not just another piece of garbage, it is fly-tying material.

Plastic T-tags lend themselves to employment on terrestrials, egg patterns and egg-sucking leeches. This T-Tag Woolly Bugger uses olive Flashabou and marabou to give the illusion of a nasty little chub stealing a trout egg from a spawning redd.

Tie this pattern with black thread on a No. 6 streamer hook. Slide a red bead on a trimmed T-tag and tie down to the hook shank. Wrap the forward end of the hook with lead. For the tail, tie in black marabou with olive Flashabou accents. Tie in a grizzly hackle tip first. Build the body with black chenille and rib with Flashabou. Wind the grizzly hackle forward and finish.

Resources

Nearest cities/towns:
Government Camp

Camping:
Frog Lake Campground

Tackle:
The Fly Fishing Shop, Welches
www.flyfishusa.com

Top Stop Food & Fuel

Visitor information:
Mt. Hood Area Chamber
www.mthood.org
503-622-3017

Midge hatches are prolific at Frog Lake, and planted trout begin to get plump by summer's end.
Photo by Robert Campbell.

Laurance Lake

Size ....127 acres

Depth..............................105 feet at the dam

Trail ....Overlooks lake

Difficulty... Moderate

Elevation ....2,980 feet

Species: Rainbow, cutthroat, bull trout

Best Methods: Fly-fishing, trolling

Tips: Bring a float tube or a boat

You are in bull trout country. It is the first sign you see at Laurance Lake. We passed it again as we started across the dam, up the Laurance Lake Loop Trail.

On the north side of the lake, the trail switchbacks up the ridge. After we gained elevation, we began to see Mount Hood in the clouds and more of the water became visible. At full pool, this lake is 127 surface acres and is over 100 feet deep at its deepest point.

Wind howled down out of the Cascades and the clouds blew through, whitecaps whipped up. Fed by the Clear Branch and Pinnacle Creek, the lake's outflow joins the Middle Fork of the Hood River.

From various vantage points we should have had a clear look at Mount Hood, but the clouds hid the glaciers and summit. We climbed on, my daughters Jennifer and Mikayla stopped to look at "fairy caves" and wildflowers. We were almost to the next switchback when I heard a high-pitched whistle. Not a marmot. A pika.

We stalked the pika for a look at the elusive animal that my girls had never seen before. We hid in vine maple and scanned a rock slide. There, perched on a rock, looking out over the mountain valley we saw him.

On the way back down, the clouds parted, the wind began to still and Hood's Langille, Coe and Ladd glaciers appeared, lit from the east.

I had borrowed a 12-foot Hobie Pro Angler kayak from Tumalo Creek Kayak and Canoe in Bend. After lunch I slipped it into the water. Mikayla was in another kayak. My dad, who had joined us for the day, pushed his pontoon boat in.

The Hobie Pro Angler can be paddled like any other kayak, but its real strength is the Mirage Drive system, which runs on a pedal system. Drop the rudder then pedal it like a bicycle. Beneath the boat, two fins kick like a merman's tail and the boat goes. A rudder control at the left hand turns the boat left and right.

This time I left the fly rod cased and tied on a crankbait. First cast. Bam. I was in bull trout country. This one was about 12 inches long.

My second fish was a hatchery rainbow. It is easy to imagine the rainbows know they are in bull trout country shortly after they go in the water. The slow ones don't make it. Once a bull trout reaches about 16 inches, it makes its living eating other fish. And a 24-inch bull can choke down an eight-inch stocker. Some big predators lurk in that lake.

Dad caught a nice rainbow on a rubber-legged Hare's Ear and, when I figured out where the fish were concentrated, I caught two more bull trout and another rainbow.

Some of the best fishing is at the mouths of the creeks, along the north shore and along the dam. Parts of the lake are protected from the wind. We found calm water off the mouth of Pinnacle Creek and along the south shore.

When I ventured around the point and into the wind chop, the Hobie did well out there too. It is a unique kayak in that a person can stand and cast. This one was equipped with a rod holder behind the seat. At first I wanted one up front then I realized I didn't need a rod holder at all. I used the paddle only in very shallow water and pedal-kicked everywhere else, my rod in my right hand, ready to set the hook.

Campground host, Ken Nelson, related a story about three anglers that didn't abide by the above-mentioned rules. Fishing with bait, they had 10 trout each in possession when the trooper fingered them earlier this season. According to Nelson, it cost each fisherman $4,350 and all their gear. Welcome to bull trout country where it pays to read the regulations.

Laurance Lake is an irrigation reservoir in the Hood River watershed near Parkdale. Thanks to regulations that restrict anglers to fly-fishing and artificial lures, this is one of the better angling lakes in the region for larger fish. Laurance is a bull trout sanctuary and it is regularly stocked by the Department of Fish and Wildlife.

Hatchery rainbow trout, native cutthroat trout and bull trout are the main catch. There are some smallmouth in the lake. Only finclipped trout and bass may be kept. Bait fishing is not permitted and anglers are not allowed to keep wild fish.

A lot of fishermen work the south shore close to camp. Best bank access is near the bridge spanning Pinnacle creek and east to the dam.

To find the most fish, pay attention to stream inlets and rocky points adjacent to deeper water.

Fly fishermen should employ a clear intermediate sinking line and a nine-foot leader. Good patterns for the lake include the Prince Nymph, Pheasant Tail, Rubber-leg Hare's Ear, Flying Ant and Woolly Bugger. To go deeper, try using a beadhead pattern and a sinking line.

Look to match hatches of Callibaetis mayflies in June. A Callibaetis nymph can produce a lot of fish in spring and early summer. The lake also has a mid-summer hatch of Hexegenia mayflies.

Resources

Nearest cities/towns:
Parkdale

Camping:
Kinnikinnick Campground

Tackle:
The Fly Fishing Shop, Welches
www.flyfishusa.com

Gorge Fly Shop

Visitor information:
Hood River County Chamber of
Commerce
www.mthood.org

A nice trail crosses the dam and winds up through the forest. Photo by Gary Lewis

To start with spinning tackle, try a 1/6-ounce Rooster Tail. Try black, brown, rainbow or frog patterns. Cast, let it sink, then retrieve. Plugs and spoons are also effective here.

Cast, tighten up the line, and crank the reel slow. Vary the depth and retrieve until you find the fish. A slow retrieve is usually the most effective.

For boaters, trolling along the north shore or dam can produce fast action. Two small boat ramps are provided on the south shore. Gas motors are not permitted.

There is a camp area on the north shore with 20 sites with no hookups. When we were there last, the camp hosts had the sites in top shape. Laurance used to be known as something of a party spot; it is once again a good place to bring the family.

Maximum RV length is 16 feet. Tables, grills, and vault toilets are provided. Bring your own drinking water.

Directions

From Highway 35, head west on Cooper Spur Road at Mount Hood Corner. Drive 4.5 miles and take a right onto Evans Creek Road. Proceed along a mostly paved road reaching the lake in five miles.

Hatchery rainbow trout, native cutthroat and bull trout make up the main catch at Laurance Lake. Photo by Mikayla Lewis

Lost Lake

Size	321 acres
Depth	167 feet
Trail	Around the lake
Difficulty	Moderate
Elevation	3,140 feet

Species ....Rainbow, brown, cutthroat, brook trout, kokanee salmon

Best Methods ....Fly-fishing, trolling, bait

Tips:
Bring a float tube or a boat

Lost Lake is surrounded by rhododendrons and dense stands of Pacific silver fir, mountain hemlock, Douglas fir, white pine and western cedar in a steep, glacier-scoured mountain valley. Formed by a lava dam, it is fed by Inlet Creek and springs on the east and west sides of the lake. Its outflow is the Lake Branch of the Hood River.

The Indians called it Heart of the Mountains, and it was a favorite camping area then as it is now. Today, we call it Lost Lake, but this popular 231-acre still water is discovered every season by travelers from all over the Northwest. Talk to the anglers and you will meet people who come back every year. And they all have tales of trophies won and lost on the water.

The lake is triangle-shaped lake and measures 3.37 miles around the perimeter. Hiking trails completely encircle the water.

The campground offers 148 sites. Tent sites cost $26 per night. Group sites are available. There are no electrical hookups. An RV dump and fill is available to RV campers. "D" Loop has RV spaces to 40 feet.

Boats are available to rent from the resort. There are two launches on the lake. A handicap-accessible fishing dock and a public launch are located on the eastern shore. Paddle as fast as you want, but no motors are allowed.

Rainbow trout are the main catch, but brown trout and kokanee are present, as well as smaller numbers of cutthroat and brook trout. ODFW supports the fishery with over 17,000 rainbows a year, including brood stock fish and surplus steelhead. Several fish in excess of eight pounds are landed each year.

At its deepest, the lake is 167 feet deep, with an average depth of 100 feet. The best trout fishing can be found in the corners and along the banks at the transitions to deeper water.

The best fishing is early in the summer. By the third week of July, the trout are well fed with bugs and grow

Lost Lake is a favorite destination for anglers from all over the West. This productive water grows big trout.

more selective. By mid-September, the trout begin to feed opportunistically again.

Large insect hatches bring the big fish into the shallows. Fly-fishermen should be prepared to match a hatch of carpenter ants in early July. Expect batches of little black mayflies (Nos. 12-14) and hexagenia mayflies (No. 6) from the middle of July to the first of August.

Spin fishermen do well with worms, salmon eggs and jar bait. A slow-trolled frog-pattern Flatfish is another favorite.

After you have caught your limit, there is a lot to do in the area. Check out the Mt. Hood Railroad from Hood River to Parkdale or go hiking in the Mt. Hood National Forest or the Columbia Gorge. Bonneville Dam is another nearby attraction. In August and early September, the berry picking can be good.

The store usually opens on May 1, but snow can keep this road sealed till early summer. Call the resort for road conditions. Check the web site for maps and updates.

Directions

From I-84 take exit 62. Turn right at Cascade Avenue. Turn right at Country Club Road. Turn left at Barrett Drive. Turn right at Tucker Road. Slight right at Dee Highway. Slight right at Lost Lake Road. Turn right at NFD 13 Road and take a slight right at NF Dev Road 1340.

From Highway 26, drive to Zig Zag. Head north on Lolo Pass Road and follow the signs to Lost Lake.

Paul's Horny Damsel
Courtesy Confluence Fly Shop

Vulnerability. That's what makes this pattern a winner. When a greedy trout sees the Horny Damsel, he'll think he's looking at a two-for-one dinner plate special. Stillwater trout begin seeing hatches of damsels in June.

Tie this pattern with black thread on a No. 10 dry fly hook. For the tail, use stiff braided line. Use white Slinky Flash for the wing and build a thorax of hare's mask to anchor the wing. A small bead can be employed to hold the wing. Tie in a pair of black mono eyes and a sparse grizzly hackle behind the eyes. Tie down the second tail at the front then again at the back. Anchor the next wing close to the front with electric blue dubbing and optional bead. Tie in mono eyes and wrap a grizzly hackle through the eyes. Color and segment the tails with markers to complete the effect.

Resources

Nearest cities/towns:
Parkdale, Dee, Hood River

Camping:
Lost Lake Resort

Tackle:
The Fly Fishing Shop, Welches
Gorge Fly Shop

Visitor information:
Hood River County Chamber of Commerce
www.mthood.org
Lost Lake Resort
www.lostlakeresort.org
541-386-6366

Olallie Lake

Size	240 acres
Depth	48 feet
Trail	Pacific Crest Trail nearby
Difficulty	Moderate
Elevation	4,941 feet

Species: Rainbow, brook trout

Best Methods: Fly-fishing, trolling, bait

Tips: Very clear water, use fluorocarbon leader.

Located just below the 5,000 foot level, off the Pacific Crest Trail, near the headwaters of the Clackamas and Breitenbush Rivers, the traveling angler finds Olallie Lake, legendary for its trophy trout. In Olallie, hatchery fish average 12 inches and the fishing can be very good, but chance for big brood trout are what make the long drive worthwhile. Olallie regularly produces trophy rainbows in the 8 to 10-pound class.

Olallie is the biggest of the 200 or so lakes that are sprinkled around the basin. It also offers some of the best fishing. This lake is easier to read than most. About a third of the water is less than 10 feet deep and numerous rocky outcroppings and points offer structure and shelter.

Head to Olallie when the snow melts in the spring. Make the drive in a high-clearance vehicle. In a year with a high snowpack, there may still be patches of snow in the road on Memorial Day weekend. Most of the action here takes place in June and July, but some of the best fishing of the year can happen late in October. At that time of year, a couple of fishermen can have the whole lake to themselves.

No motors are allowed on the lake and swimming is not allowed. The lake provides the drinking water for the resort and campgrounds. There are three campgrounds on Olallie's shores and several others in the vicinity. Food should be stored in coolers in vehicles and not left in tents or around camp. There are a lot of black bears in the area. Bring mosquito repellent, the marshy meadows above the lake produce a lot of bugs.

Olallie's rainbows are taken on slow-trolled Thomas spoons, Rooster Tail spinners and Power Bait. Fly fishermen score with black leech patterns, callibaetis nymphs, caddis and chironomid patterns.

The most popular bank fishing spot is on the north

Olallie Lake is legendary for big rainbows. From ice-out through October an angler has a shot at catching a limit or a trout that could tip the scales at ten pounds.

Resources

Nearest cities/towns:
Detroit, Estacada, Government Camp

Camping:
Ollalie Lake Resort

Tackle:
Ollalie Lake Resort
The Fly Fishing Shop, Welches
Estacada Tackle

Visitor information:
www.olallielakeresort.com
www.estacadachamber.org
www.mthood.org
www.fs.fed.us

Mt. Jefferson as seen from Olallie Lake. Photo by Gary Lewis

end of the lake, west of the resort. It is close to the road where a big rock wall slopes down into the water. Big trout can be glimpsed cruising the bank.

This is a good spot to still-fish as well, or pull flies in a kick-boat. Both the east bank and the west bank have good shallows and structure and are good for trollers. Other good still-fishing spots can be found in the narrows off Peninsula Campground.

A lot of hikers pass through the area on the Pacific Crest Trail. There are trailheads nearby that lead to Olallie Butte and to Twin Peaks. A trail encircles the lake. Hikers that bring a container can pick buckets full of blueberries in the early fall.

A number of lakes in the area offer good hike-in or drive-to fishing. Try Horseshoe Lake from the road south of Olallie. From the trailhead at Olallie, the uphill climb can lead to Timber Lake or Upper Lake. Lower Lake can be reached from a trailhead north of Olallie. These lakes are stocked with fingerling rainbows every other year. A spinning rod rigged with a float and fly setup is a good choice for these smaller lakes.

Directions

From Government Camp, head east on U.S. Highway 26 then turn south on Forest Service Road 42. Proceed 32 miles south on 42 and 4220.

Pine Hollow Reservoir

Size	240 acres
Depth	15 feet (average)
Difficulty	Easy
Elevation	2,200 feet

Species: Rainbow, largemouth, bluegill, bullhead

Best Methods: Fly fishing, trolling, bait

Tips: Plan to fish in April, May, June, September and October

Pine Hollow Reservoir is a pretty, popular irrigation reservoir set in a forest of mixed pines and oaks, west of Tygh Valley. Less than two hours drive from Portland or Bend and less than an hour away from The Dalles, it attracts plenty of attention on spring and summer weekends. For good reason. The Department of Fish and Wildlife makes sure that there are plenty of trout in the water, including a number of big brood stock rainbows. Trout average 10 inches with holdovers running to 16 inches. The lake has produced rainbows that have stretched the tape to 32 inches.

We last fished Pine Hollow Reservoir in late October. With hunting seasons in full swing and the summer splash and giggle set back in school, it was a good time to hit the water. It didn't hurt that ODFW had recently planted the lake with legal rainbows.

We set out from the public launch, kicking away in our float tubes. Within minutes, Pete Chadwell had hooked the first fish. He landed two more in the next 20 minutes. It took Nolan King and Jesse Short and I a little bit longer to get started, but soon we had cracked the code and we began to catch fish too. My choice that day was a 4-weight Orvis Helios rod with a slow-sink line. I tied on a beadhead leech with a peacock body, red hackle and a blood red marabou tail. Using a slow-twitch troll from my Caddis Navigator IV, I hooked and landed several.

Largemouth bass grow big here, as well. Five-pounders are not uncommon. From June through September, the reservoir's bluegills and catfish provide good sport for warmwater fisherman.

Many of the biggest fish are taken on Power Bait. Use a sliding sinker to a barrel swivel and 28 inches of leader terminating at a No. 14 treble hook. Mold a Power Bait nugget around the hook. The bait will float off the bottom. Leave a little slack in the line and set the hook when the line starts to move.

Trolling accounts for a lot of the rainbows that are taken every year. Anglers have success with Thomas Buoyant spoons and Kwikfish in rainbow, tiger and silver/blue color schemes. Try a zigzag trolling pattern through the buoy line. Another good trolling area is in the northwest corner near Camp Morrow.

Best fishing from the bank is on either side of the

Pete Chadwell plays a rainbow trout at Pine Hollow Reservoir. Photo by Gary Lewis

east shore boat ramp. At the south shore boat ramp, bank access can be found west of the ramp. Use Rooster Tail spinners or plunk Power Bait. When the water is calm, use a bobber and worm or Pautzke's Balls-O-Fire salmon eggs. Experiment with leader length until you find the proper depth.

Two boat ramps are available, one on the east side and the other on the south shore. A 10-mph speed limit is enforced for most of the year. Waterskiing is permitted on the west half of the lake from July 1 through Labor Day. Motorboats, pontoon boats, paddleboats and jet skis are available for rental from the resort. If you bring your own boat, you can rent a spot at the dock.

Lakeside Resort and RV Park, on the east shore, is your best bet for camping at Pine Hollow. Campsites are rented by the day or the week. Toilets, showers, and water are provided. RV sites have water, electric and sewer hookups. Cabins and A-Frames are available by the day or week. At the General Store, you'll find snacks, fuel, fishing tackle and propane. Next door is Angler's Restaurant & Lounge with a view of the water.

Lakeside Resort hosts a fishing derby during the last week in April and a kid's derby on Free Fishing Weekend in June. Contact the resort for details.

Directions

From Highway 216, head west on Tygh Valley Road. Proceed into Wamic and turn left on Wamic Market Road (between storage building and tavern). Drive for 4 miles, then turn right on Ross Road. Proceed 3.5 miles and turn left at the intersection.

Bloodworm
Tied by Pete Ouelette

When trout are feeding opportunistic high in the water column, they are vulnerable to a searching pattern like a Bloodworm. This bug is imitative of the larval stage of the chironomid midge as it moves up from the mud at the bottom of the lake. The tail is meant to be an extension of the body, undulating as it wriggles through the water.

Midges don't move fast. Use a S-L-O-W one-inch retrieve or keep it still on a tight floating line. Use a small strike indicator or watch for the end of the line to stab toward the middle of the lake.

Tie the Bloodworm with red thread on a No. 12-14 long hook. For the tail, use red marabou. Build the body with red floss silk and rib with fluorescent red floss. Finish with a head of bronze peacock herl.

Fishing from his Caddis Navigator IV Gary Lewis lands a rainbow that fell for a leech pattern.
Photo by Pete Chadwell

Rock Creek Reservoir

Size	90 acres
Depth	34 feet
Difficulty	Easy
Elevation	2,200 feet

Species: Rainbow, largemouth, bluegill, bullhead

Best Methods: Fly fishing, trolling, bait

Tips: Plan to fish early in the season

This irrigation reservoir in north Central Oregon is at its best early in the season. The Department of Fish and Wildlife stocks approximately 12,000 legal rainbow trout from April through May. When the snow begins to melt up on the mountain, the fishing can be hot at Rock Creek Reservoir.

The trout average ten to twelve inches, but holdover fish grow to 18 inches and beyond. It is common for ODFW to plant larger brood stock fish that run five to eight pounds.

The lake is fed by both Rock Creek (on the north end) and Wildcat Creek. These arms are particularly productive early in the season when rainbows feed in the shallows. Look for callibaetis may flies in late May and June and be ready with a selection of ant patterns in case the wind blows Hymenoptera onto the water.

Try to time the fishing for either early or late in the day when the fish are close to the surface. When the sun is high in the sky, target trout in deeper water. All methods work well here. Bait is allowed and anglers in pontoon boats or row boats can take fish trolling Rapalas or plugs. Bank anglers will do the best when using jar baits.

Look for largemouth bass near tall grass and shoreside willows and around rocky points.

Bluegill can be found in the shallows near structure, especially around the willows, weedbeds and clumps of grass. For bluegill use small wet flies or cast dries to rising fish.

For the best bank access fish from the north shore or the dam. Prospect the shallows east of the dam

Rock Creek Reservoir shines brightest in the spring before irrigation draws off the water. Rainbow and largemouth are the main target species here.

for warmwater fish.

A small ramp on the south end of the lake is suitable for small boats. Gas motors are not permitted on the lake.

Within the campground you will find 33 basic sites with no hookups. Maximum length is 18 feet. Picnic tables, grills, pit toilets, and drinking water are provided.

Plan the trip for April or May. Early in the spring, Rock Creek Reservoir is a pleasant place to spend a day. Summer drawdown starts in late June and by mid-July the water is low and the fishing experience begins to suffer.

Directions

Start at Tygh Valley, head six miles west on Tygh Valley and Wamic Market Roads. From Wamic, head west on Rock Creek Dam Road for a bit over miles. Then head west on Forest Road 4820, and turn right on Forest Road 120. Follow signs to boat launch.

Resources

Nearest cities/towns:
Wamic, Tygh Valley, Maupin

Camping:
Rock Creek

Tackle:
Wamic Country Store
541-544-2333

The Fly Fishing Shop, Welches

Deschutes Canyon Fly Shop
www.flyfishingdeschutes.com

Deschutes Angler Fly Shop
www.deschutesangler.com

Visitor information:
Mt. Hood Area Chamber
www.mthood.org
503-622-3017

Gary Lewis Outdoors pro staffer Tommy Brown fishing from the dam at Rock Creek Reservoir. Photo by Gary Lewis

Rocky Ridge Ranch

Size:
Mule's Ear Lake.................................15 acres
Wild Rose Lake ....20 acres
Mullein Lake.....................................25 acres

Maximum Depth:
Mule's Ear Lake................................ 25 feet
Wild Rose Lake .... 30 feet
Mullein Lake..................................... 60 feet

Regulations......................... Catch & Release

Difficulty... Easy Access

Elevation.. 2,200 feet

Species: Rainbow trout

Best Methods: Fly fishing

Tips: Plan the trip with a local fly shop or fly fishing club for intelligence on fly patterns and methods.

High on a plateau between the mountain and the canyon of the Deschutes sits Rocky Ridge Ranch. This working cattle operation raises black Angus and orchard grass. Here the ground is watered with irrigation from Boulder Creek and White River and some of that glacial goodness is put to work to grow big rainbow trout.

Rocky Ridge Ranch has long been a private pay-for-access destination for fly-rodders in the know. Now under new ownership the lakes may be reserved through fly shops or on-line. Want the inside scoop? Book through a fly shop whose owners and/or employees have personally fished Rocky Ridge. They will know which flies to tie dependent on the season and hatches in progress.

There are three lakes in play. All three are stocked with Kamloops and redband rainbows. Here the trout average about 22 inches and the biggest fish run to 30 inches.

Mule's Ear, at 15 surface acres is the smallest lake and the first encountered when one drives through the gate. Mule's Ear is 25 feet deep at the dam.

Wild Rose has 20 surface acres and reaches a maximum depth of 30 feet. There is a cabin on the west end of the lake. A small timber-framed structure, the Wild Rose cabin was built with lumber harvested and milled on-site. The cabin sleeps up to six people and is furnished with electricity, flush toilet, shower, all cooking utensils and sheets on the beds. Bring your own bedding.

At 25 acres with a depth of 60 feet, Mullein Lake

is the largest body of water on the ranch. It is also the lowest in the chain and the most-protected when the wind blows. Mullein is characterized by cattails and tules at the inlet and rocky cliff walls where winter runoff helps to fill the reservoir. Of course, the deepest water is at the dam. There is a day shed with restrooms and a cooking area at Mullein Lake and a camping/parking area suitable for an RV.

To fish Rocky Ridge Ranch, bring a 5wt to 7wt rod with a matching reel and 100 yards of backing. It is important to have two lines, a floating and an intermediate (slow-sinking line). For leaders, bring 9- to 10-footers with 4x tippet for dry flies and 3x tippet for wet flies.

Best patterns for fishing subsurface, are Seal Buggers, Woolly Buggers and other leech patterns in olive, black and red. For fishing close to the reeds and in and around weed beds, use snail patterns like the Renegade (dry or wet) and the Brown Hackle (unweighted). Callibaetis nymphs, damsel nymphs, dragonfly nymphs and chironomid patterns are important.

Attractor dries like No. 12 Red Tarantula, Sparkle PMX and Stimulators can bring trout to the top when fish are feeding opportunistically. Both dragonfly and damselfly dries can produce in late spring and summer.

The lakes may close in the summer to protect the trout from heat stress. When the water cools again in September, grasshopper patterns like the Schroeder's Hopper are in play. Be sure to have a selection of Flying Ants to match bugs that may blow onto the

The view from the cabin at Wild Rose Lake.
Photo by Gary Lewis

Resources

Nearest cities/towns:
Wamic, Tygh Valley, Maupin

Camping:
RV, tent or rent cabin

Tackle:
Wamic Country Store
541-544-2333

The Fly Fishing Shop, Welches

Deschutes Canyon Fly Shop
www.flyfishingdeschutes.com

Deschutes Angler Fly Shop
www.deschutesangler.com

Visitor information:
Mt. Hood Area Chamber
www.mthood.org
503-622-3017

Mullein Lake is characterized by rocky ridges and terrain features that make this a very interesting stillwater to fish. Photo by Gary Lewis

water in big numbers.

It's a good idea to have waders and an oversize landing net. Although the weather is often good, bring raingear and layer with fleece in case there is a chill in the air. Polarized glasses are a good idea.

Some anglers prefer to fish from shore and access to the waterline is good in places on all three lakes. With its multiple arms and rocky ridges, Mullein might offer the best shore fishing. Many anglers bring float tubes or pontoon boats, but canoes and kayaks are also at home on these waters. Car top aluminum boats, drift boats or prams are welcome as well. It's a good idea to clean the boat before and after fishing to make sure to not transfer invasive species. Nice launches at each lake make it easy to trailer-in a boat.

With the exception of harvest season, the communities of Wamic and Smock Prairie are peaceful and quiet and, in the rain shadow of Wy'east, it could be wet in Portland while it is dry in ranch country.

On average there are 177 sunny days per year in Wamic, while the number of days with any precipitation is 87 (154 precipitation days in Portland). Wamic's annual rainfall measures 16.2 inches while the region sees 54.9 inches of snow.

Directions

There are four main routes to reach the ranch. Some are open dependent on the weather. The Tygh Valley approach is the most reliable in all conditions.

From Highway 26 take OR-216 (18 east of Government Camp) and drive for 15 miles. Turn left on US-197 toward The Dalles. Turn left at yellow light and drive into Tygh Valley. Turn right on Wamic Market Road and follow signs to Wamic, 5.8 miles. Bear left on Wamic Market Road into the town of Wamic. Turn left on Smock Road at the edge of town. Continue on Smock Road until the pavement ends.

The address is Rocky Ridge Ranch, 54829 Smock Road, Wamic, Oregon. Additional directions are on the web site at www.rockyridgeranchoregon.com

Smock Prairie Reservoir

Size	20 acres
Depth	50 feet
Trail	½ mile
Difficulty	Easy
Elevation	2,146 feet

Species: Rainbow, largemouth

Best Methods: Bait

Tips: This lake is usually stocked in late May

Scrappy rainbow trout wait for you at this north-central Oregon impoundment.

It's a good sign when you draw a strike with your first few casts, so I was pretty jazzed when the Dick Nite spoon got hit and hit hard on only the third try. The chunky ten-inch rainbow immediately took to the air, but couldn't shake the little spoon. I quickly banked him, and he became the first of a good number of rainbows we would string up that day. A hot summer day yielded plenty of trout from 6 to 14 inches, all against a scenic backdrop of rocky hills and woods.

Reminiscent of Ozark Mountain lakes, the Smock Prairie Reservoir is nestled between rugged hills and shady groves of live oak on the White River Wildlife Area. It lies along the southern edge of the Smock Prairie Flat just north of the White River Canyon. Mostly a local secret and often referred to as "Miller's Pond," this quiet lake in the shadow of Mount Hood draws only a few visitors, even on weekends. It is stocked regularly by the ODFW with keeper sized rainbows, and the clear water is deep enough and cold enough to offer summer refuge. That means there are some larger hold-over trout in addition to the stockers.

The lake's shady, clear banks are a perfect place for families to gather, do a little fishing, and enjoy a picnic. The half-mile hike to the lake wanders through woods of pine and oak, and is easy enough for a six-year old child. And, the bank fishing is easy.

Most regulars offer the trout prepared baits like Powerbait or salmon eggs, and worms. They can be fished below a float, or along the bottom. As we found out, the scrappy rainbows will also readily take small spoons and spinners. Bronze blades seem to be the most effective.

As in most trout lakes, the fish will be close to the surface early in the day, and will drop deeper as the sun climbs. They come back up at sunset.

This is a perfect lake for a float tube excursion and a fly rod, especially in the morning and evening when the fish gather near the surface. Most tried and true general trout patterns will work on these hatchery-raised rainbows.

Nestled among the hills and surrounded by oak trees, Smock Prairie Reservoir might remind the traveling angler of an Ozark mountain lake. Photo by Terry Otto

The trout are scattered over the lake, but a few spots tend to draw them on a regular basis. Look near the inlet of the irrigation water which feeds the lake along the south shore. The dam is another good place to find trout, and the northern bank right near the dam is good, too.

Directions

From State Highway 216 take Victor Road north to the White River Crossing Road, which will take you north over the White River Canyon. Smock Road will take you to the White River WA parking lot and trailhead. There is a rough road to the lake that is closed from three days prior to Memorial Day, and opens again after Labor Day. An ODFW wildlife area parking permit must be displayed on the dash.

Maps of the wildlife area are available at the wildlife area headquarters: (541) 544-2126

There are few local amenities, but gas, groceries, and some fishing gear are available at the Wamic Country Store just a few miles away.

It took only three casts for the author to hook and land this Smock Reservoir rainbow. Most trout in the lake run 6 to 14 inches, but there are a few larger trout as well. Photo by Terry Otto

Iridescent Black Cricket
Tied by Dave Miller

If you like beating up on September trout and panfish with a hopper, change it up a bit next time you head to the stream. Here's a great cricket pattern taken from Probasco's Favorite Northwest Flies by Frank Amato Publications.

You can catch fish on grasshopper and cricket imitations all summer long, but there's something about September that makes fish pull in close to the bank and watch the current for terrestrials on top. Dead drift the Iridescent Black Cricket along grassy banks all the way till dark. It's okay to give it a little twitch now and then.

Tie this pattern with black thread on a No. 10 Daiichi 1270. For the tail, use black stripped quills. For the abdomen, use black #202 Foamback, wound around the hook. To make the legs, use dyed black pheasant tail, knotted at the knees. Build the wing and head from a section of dyed black turkey feather. For the antenna, use stripped grizzly hackle stems. Use black beads or melted mono for the eyes. For the thorax, use black iridescent dubbing. Pull the turkey quill forward, secure behind the eyes and trim off excess. Pick out the dubbing with a bodkin.

Resources

Nearest cities/towns:
Wamic, Tygh Valley, Maupin

Camping:
Mt. Hood National Forest

Tackle:
Wamic Country Store
541-544-2333

The Fly Fishing Shop, Welches

Deschutes Canyon Fly Shop
www.flyfishingdeschutes.com

Deschutes Angler Fly Shop
www.deschutesangler.com

Visitor information:
Mt. Hood Area Chamber
www.mthood.org
503-622-3017

Twin Lakes

Size:
Upper Twin ....11 acres
Lower Twin ....18 acres

Maximum Depth:
Upper Twin .... 4 feet
Lower Twin .... 18 feet

Trail ....Trailhead is at Frog Lake Sno-Park, approx. 7 miles east of Government Camp on Hwy. 26, well-marked.

Hike .... Approx. 2 miles to Lower Twin from trailhead, about another mile to Upper Twin Lake. Moderate elevation gains.

Elevation:
Upper Twin .... 4,288 feet
Lower Twin .... 4,185 feet
Trailhead .... 3,900 feet

Species: Brook trout

Best Methods: Fly, bait or lure

Tips: Focus your angling attention on Lower Twin Lake; Upper Twin is extremely shallow and often winter kills.

Twin Lakes are a couple of hike-in waters relatively close to the Metro area where the angler short on time might sneak away for a quick hike and a few hours of fishing. The hike begins at Frog Lake Sno-park where you pick up the Pacific Crest Trail No. 2,000. Along with all other trailheads in the Mt. Hood National Forest, a Forest Pass is required to park here.

The PCT gradually climbs for about 1-1/2 miles through a beautiful Douglas fir forest before reaching the junction with Twin Lakes Trail No. 495. This section of the PCT is wide and fairly smooth, making it kid and pet-friendly. It is also popular for hikers with horses and llamas. During winter this section of trail is widely used for snowshoeing. In summer, watch for bear grass, Indian paintbrush, lupine and rhododendron along the trail.

Up to the junction with Twin Lakes Trail you will likely be vexed by the sound of jake brakes from trucks negotiating nearby Wapinitia Pass, but as you drop over the ridge on trail No. 495 and begin the descent into Lower Twin Lake, you leave the sounds of the modern world behind you. It's another half-mile to Lower Twin on trail No. 495.

At the bottom of the hill, a short spur trail descends from No. 495 down to the lake on the south end. For the overnight angler, there are several good camp spots to choose from in this area, though there are no facilities. No trace camping techniques are advised.

A fisherman's trail encircles the lake and provides access for anglers and adventurous children. There is a history of raft-building at Lower Twin, but use these

The beautiful green water at Lower Twin Lake is as welcoming for a swim as it is for trout fishing during the heat of the summer. Photo by Gary Lewis.

craft at your own risk—some of them are of dubious construction. The gray jays at Lower Twin Lake are savvy to visitors' trail mix, so don't be surprised if one lands on your head while looking for a handout.

Both Lower and Upper Twin Lakes are stocked every other year with brook trout. The trout grow well in each lake but have a tough time surviving the winters at Upper Twin due to the shallow water. On multiple visits to Upper Twin during the summer of 2014, I neither caught any fish nor saw any sign of their presence. ODFW continues to stock Upper Twin at this time, but angling up there is a roll-of-the-dice affair.

Fishing at Lower Twin can be quite good at times despite the pressure it receives. Being such a pretty little place so close to town, and with such an easy hike in, it is quite popular. The brook trout here average a respectable 9-11 inches, and with ample shallows in the north and south end to support the food chain, Lower Twin's brook trout can be quite plump by the end of a productive summer feeding on damselfly nymphs, midges and mayflies. I am always amazed at the number of damselflies present here during the summer months, and a No. 8 or No. 10 olive marabou damsel nymph fished on a clear intermediate fly line can be deadly in June and July. Occasionally some larger brookies up to 14 or 15-inches are caught here, but they are rare.

If you arrive to Lower Twin early in the season when there is still snow on the ground, the trout are ravenous and will readily strike small spoons and spinners, as well as bait. Later in the summer, however, the trout here become accustomed to natural forage and get tougher to catch, even for fly fishermen. In fact, if you visit Lower Twin on a sunny summer day in July or August, you might swear there are no fish here as fishing during mid-day can be slow. More so than any other high lake I have ever fished, the fish in Lower Twin often go completely off the bite during mid-day. No worries. Go explore during the day and focus your angling efforts to the evening and early morning hours.

It is easy to fish from shore with spinning gear at Lower Twin, but a bit tougher with a fly rod. Fly fishermen will enjoy the freedom that a Caddis float tube affords for casting. In fact, one of my favorite tactics is kicking along the east or west shorelines throwing dry flies to within inches of the bank in the low light of morning or evening. Most of the west shore drops off steeply into deep water which gives the trout security. On the east shore there are lots of logs and brush that afford the fish cover while feeding. The shallows on both the north and south ends of the lake can come alive with feeding activity in the fading light of a summer evening.

One beautiful feature of Lower Twin Lake is the amazing color of its water. When the bright summer sun strikes Lower Twin at the correct angle, the lake glows a brilliant aquamarine color. Coincidentally, the brook trout here often have a glowing blue-green hue to the worm markings on their back, making them some of the most gorgeous brook trout to be seen. During the heat of the summer, the pure waters of this lake are quite welcoming for a swim, and many people come here just for that reason.

While Upper Twin Lake might be a bust for angling on any given year, it is still worth a visit if just for the invigorating hike. The trail from Lower to Upper Twin is narrow at times and has a few steeper sections, but is still fairly easy. Upper Twin is incredibly scenic with a nice view of Mt. Hood looming over the north end. You can follow Upper Twin Lake Trail No. 533 for about a quarter-mile around the east side of the lake to the Palmateer Trail No. 482. Follow this rugged little trail for some excellent views of Mt. Hood and Barlow Butte, but keep a close eye on the kids as there are cliffs at a couple of viewpoints along this track.

Resources

Nearest cities/towns:
Government Camp

Accommodations:
Government Camp resorts

Camping:
Mt. Hood National Forest

Tackle:
The Fly Fishing Shop, Welches

Visitor information:
Mt. Hood Area Chamber
www.mthood.org
503-622-3017

Reading List

On Mount Hood
A Biography of Oregon's Perilous Peak
By Jon Bell

Hatch Guide for the Lower Deschutes River
Frank Amato Publications
By Jim Schollmeyer

Oregon Lake Maps & Fishing Guide
Frank Amato Publications
By Gary Lewis

Oregon River Maps & Fishing Guide
Frank Amato Publications

FISHING Central Oregon
By Hill, Lewis, Snavely, Wing

Fishing in Oregon
By Flying Pencil

Fishing Oregon's Deschutes River
By Scott Richmond

A River in the Sun (a novel)
By Scott Richmond

Illustrated Rigging for Salmon Steelhead & Trout
By Robert H. Campbell

Hiking Mount Hood Nat'l Forest
By Marcia Sinclair

Kingsley Reservoir

Size	60 acres
Depth	20 feet
Difficulty	Easy
Elevation	3.165 feet

Species: Rainbow trout

Best Methods: Bait, trolling

Tips: Also known as Upper Green Point Reservoir

If you like to combine motorsports with your fishing, then Kingsley Reservoir is the place for you. On any weekend during the spring, you'll find motorcyclists and four-wheelers climbing the hill and going over jumps and roaring around on various trails through the brush. And most of them are fishermen. After they run out of gas, they head down to the water.

Though the environment is noisy, the fishing can be good. The Department of Fish and Wildlife stocks Kingsley (also known as Green Point Reservoir) with 10,000 legal rainbows. This is one of those lakes you can fish well from the bank. The best access is at the dam where the water averages about 20 feet deep. To get away from the crowd, walk across the dam around to the west side of the lake.

Bait fishing is popular here and trolling accounts for a lot of fish. In the deep water by the dam, where most of the bait fishing takes place, you can catch fish on a brown Rooster Tail or a Mack's Lure Promise Keeper spinner. Cast, let it sink, give it a twitch and retrieve. Keep the spinner moving fast enough to keep the blade revolving, but don't reel so fast that you spook the trout. There are a few snags out there, but that's the price you pay for hard strikes and fast limits. Fish average 10 inches and holdovers can run to 15 inches.

Jar baits are popular on Kingsley, but bait fishing with nightcrawlers and Pautzke's is just as productive. Use a No. 10 single bait hook and about three feet of leader beneath your float or bobber.

If you have a small boat, there's a launch near the dam that you can use. There is no dock and the parking area is not paved, nor is it marked. Motors are permitted on the lake. Try slow-trolling a flasher

Even in low water, Kingsley Reservoir can kick out a fast limit of trout. Photo by Jake Carse

rig tipped with a nightcrawler or pull a small wobbling plug in a rainbow, frog, or crayfish pattern.

Lower Green Point Reservoir can be found downhill, north of the lake. A road follows the eastern shore.

Mixed age stands of firs, and maples surround Kingsely Reservoir. Ferns and huckleberries grow in the openings. The campground is open and primitive with about 20 unmarked spots. There are no hookups. Some groups arrange their RVs in a circle to protect against wind and weather. The campsites are suitable for smaller RVs and tents. A few tables and a toilet are provided. Use existing fire rings. There is no drinking water.

Directions

Drive from Hood River to Oak Grove. From Oak Grove's Reed Road, proceed west on Binns Hill Drive. Turn left on Kingsley Road and follow for six miles to the reservoir. The road goes up, up, up, through a tree farm. Be cautious, the road is a single lane with turnouts.

Jar baits and spinners can be real productive at Kingsley but these trout will take a fly, too. Photo by Jake Carse

Jake Carse walked down to the water's edge caught a trout on the first cast. Photo by Jake Carse

Flay's Cray
Tied by James Flaherty

For smallmouth, for trout and for carp, it pays to have a small selection of crayfish imitations. Flay's Cray is an easy tie with the profile, color and flash to attract the attention of a predator. I like that it uses a red tag as a strike trigger.

A crawdad pattern is worthless unless it is weighted to sink right to the bottom. When plumbing the depths for trout or smallmouth bass, fish these imitations like any other streamer with long strips and long pauses.

Tie this pattern with brown thread on a No. 2 4x long streamer hook. Start with 10 or more wraps of .025 lead wire. At the back of the hook, wrap a red wool tag and then tie in split squirrel tail fibers dyed rust. Tie in orange or black rubber nymph legs for antennae and six strands of copper Krystal Flash - three on each side. Wrap the body with peacock sparkle chenille and overlay with rusty brown dubbing. Tie in large dumbbell eyes and finish with a few turns of olive dubbing.

Resources

Nearest cities/towns:
Hood River

Camping:
Primitive

Tackle:
The Fly Fishing Shop, Welches
Gorge Fly Shop

Visitor information:
Hood River County Chamber of Commerce
www.hoodriver.org

Navigating to a Remote Lake

A fishing partner phoned to tell me about an outstanding backcountry lake. The lake is pristine with little pressure and is worth the effort to get there. While the fishing is good, the trek to the lake is a challenge.

I ask myself, "How do I navigate to the lake? What is the simplest method that pairs my map and compass to a Global Positioning System (GPS) receiver?"

If my friend doesn't know the exact latitude and longitude coordinates, hopefully he can give me a general description or name of the lake. I call him back and he sends me to Rim Lake, nestled in the Three Sisters Wilderness just north of the iconic Broken Top Mountain.

I begin my route planning with both my wilderness map and free online mapping programs, such as Gmap4 (www.mappingsupport.com) and Google Maps (www.earth.google.com.) How easy- I just type in "Rim Lake, Oregon" in the search bar.

Looking closely at the details on the topo map, I find that there are no trails in the vicinity of the lake; I will have to go off-trail. Directly northwest of Rim Lake is Park Meadow, an easy hike from the Park Meadow Trailhead. I notice the contour lines (brown lines) are fairly wide apart, and I look for potential routes where I can bushwhack my way fairly comfortably from point to point.

Mapping programs provide the coordinates of my point-to-point locations that will be used for setting waypoints These coordinates will help me navigate safely from the Park Meadow trailhead to the meadow itself and then on to Rim Lake. Because I have to go off-trail to Rim Lake, I take the time to review the topo map in detail to assess the overall big picture. I must determine the safest route, find

and identify natural obstacles, and evaluate terrain features. Thankfully, the elevation gain is moderate.

My first step is to ensure the GPS coordinates match those of the map I am using. I do so by selecting my GPS receiver's "set-up" icon, I then verify the default settings are in degrees and minutes. I can always change coordinates later if need be.

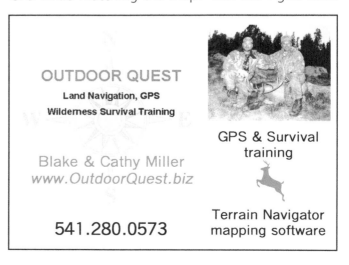

Depending on which GPS receiver model I decide to use, I select the "mark" button from the main menu. I move the back-lighted bar up to coordinates and select "enter" or edit. After entering my point to point coordinates I select "save" or "done." Now I move the back-lighted bar up to the waypoint default number and give it a name - RIM. Finally, I select the "save" or "done" icon at the bottom of the Mark Waypoint page.

After entering the coordinates, I mentally review my data entry process. These new waypoints will determine whether I find that lake or not. Did I enter multiple point-to-point coordinates in my GPS while matching the map? Yes. Did I give each waypoint a distinct, identifiable name? Yes. And most importantly, did I verify that each of my newly entered waypoints was saved to my GPS memory? This can be done quickly by selecting "Find" or the "GO To" icon and then reviewing all waypoints. If the waypoint RIM and all of the other names I assigned are displayed then I am ready to navigate.

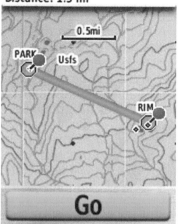

My GPS receiver is now displaying my route from the waypoints that are entered (below).

To navigate from Park Meadow to Rim Lake, I select "Find" and "Waypoints." From the list of waypoints, I select "RIM" and then select "GO."

I now page through the various navigation screens and select the "Compass" option.

My GPS provides direction (125° True) and distance (1.06 miles) to the waypoint "RIM." The red arrow provides a visual cue and points to the physical location of the waypoint "RIM." As I move off-trail through the backcountry, the GPS receiver provides continuous updates to the selected waypoint destination. As I move closer to the lake, my pace may cause the red arrow to rotate and the digital information to change. Wanting to do nothing but get my line in the water and enjoy the seclusion of Rim Lake, I use the map page to corroborate the electronic compass information.

Dave Kilhefner with a wild steelhead.
Photo by Dave Kilhefner

Shore breakfast. Photo by Gary Lewis

Gary's clothing provided by Guide's Choice.
Photo by Travis Huisman

Fly-fishing Gear and Strategy

For most applications, the rod should be eight to nine feet long and it should be equipped with as many line guides as it is long. Example given: a nine foot rod should have at least nine guides.

The rod is classified by line weight, length and action. The weight of rod should be dependent on the type of fishing anticipated. When fishing small, slow-moving waters where the fish average eight to fourteen inches, a four or five weight rod should be adequate. If the angler alternates between fishing for small stream trout and stillwaters where the fish grow a little bigger, a five or six weight rod may be in order.

If low-water steelhead is the primary target, a six-weight would be a good choice. In heavier water, where bigger fish may be encountered, a seven weight is appropriate. An eight or nine weight is preferred in bigger water or when salmon are the quarry.

A fast action is a good choice for the dry fly fisherman. This is also a good choice for someone who prefers stream fishing. Stillwater anglers often prefer a medium to slow action rod when bigger fish may be encountered.

The primary function of the reel is to hold line. Most fish under fifteen inches are not played on the reel. Rather, the fisherman gains line by pulling it in with the off hand. When larger fish are more often encountered, the fisherman should consider higher quality reels that are balanced and equipped with a high-quality drag to slow down a running fish.

Beginners should start with a floating line, matched to the weight of the rod. Since the fly itself is nearly weightless, the line serves as the weight needed to cast the fly.

Besides weight, fly lines are also classified as to their shape. A double taper (DT) is tapered at both ends of the line and may be the best choice in small stream presentations where casting long distances is not an issue. The weight forward (WF) line is the best choice for steelhead and salmon fishermen and anyone else who needs to cast long distances. With the weight forward line, finesse is traded for distance. Each angler will have to make his own decision.

The leader connects the fly to the end of the fly line and is often ignored by newcomers to the sport as unimportant. It is very important to match the right leader to the fly and fish. In most cases, the leader should be tapered, starting with a heavy butt section, graduating to lighter, more supple sections, culminating in a tippet section that is tied to the fly.

Proper coordination of leader and fly will result in well-placed casts, proper action imparted to the fly and, hopefully, more fish brought to hand.

Commercial knotless tapered leaders come in 7-1/2 feet, 9 feet and 12 feet. The beginner should match the leader to the length of the rod, but eventually, the size you want to use will be dictated on fish and conditions.

Casting

Casting lessons can start inside with a fly rod tip section and a length of thick yarn. The rod is brought from one o'clock to eleven o'clock. The yarn's weight and bulk simulate fly line action. Before starting the back cast, wait until the line straightens out. Come back to one o'clock. WAIT until the line straightens out behind you before beginning the forward cast.

Once the yarn presentation is mastered, the novice fly angler has the basics of fly-casting licked. It is time to graduate to a real rod in the backyard loaded with a reel, backing, line, leader and hookless yarn "fly".

Mark out a spot in the yard and practice casting the fly to it. At the end of the back cast "pull", let your wrist "break" at the one o'clock mark, allowing the rod to incline toward vertical. STOP at the end of each "pull" and "push" stroke, forcing the rod to work.

This is called false casting. On the stream, it is used to air-dry the fly and feed line into the cast.

With your off hand, pull line from the reel, feeding it into the loop you are casting.

Watch other fly fishermen. What are they doing wrong? What are they doing right? Concentrate on improving your form and precision. Longer casting will follow form.

To fish small streams, learn the simple pick-up-and-lay down, the roll cast and how to dap (dangle the fly from the tip of the rod to the surface of the water). All these casts may be learned in an hour of practice.

Once you have mastered a few casts, you are ready to fish. You can learn more about casting by finding yourself a teacher. Most fly shops are eager to help a newcomer to the sport.

Some Strategies

The best teacher is the stream itself, preferably a small stream with pocket water and eager trout. In a typical freestone creek or small river, the water creates a cyclic pattern of riffles, runs and pools.

The riffle is the fastest moving portion of any section of stream. It may average from six inches to six feet deep depending on water flow and size of the stream. It has a bottom of gravel, boulder or smooth stones.

Downstream from the riffle, the action of the water has carved out a run. The water slows and the stream widens.

The run becomes a pool. On a slow-moving stream, the pool will be far wider than the riffles and run.

Where do you fish? Spend some time watching the stream. Note the smooth spots in the run that indicate a submerged boulder. Look for underwater features that divert current and disrupt flow. Look for external components, such as overhanging banks, fallen trees and bridges that provide shade and protection for fish.

When fishing for stream trout, remember that the stream brings food to the fish. Think about where a fish is most likely to feed. Where can the fish rest, yet watch the current that brings him his dinner?

The riffle concentrates the food, but also concentrates the current, making it costly in terms of energy to feed for long in a riffle. The biggest trout will often be found where the concentration of food coincides with the end of the riffle and the beginning of a slower current.

Watch the stream and look for feeding fish. Dry flies are most often fished to imitate the downstream drift of a fallen or hatching insect. Seek to match the size, shape and color of the natural insects you find streamside. If there are no insects to be found, fish an attractor fly like the Royal Coachman or Renegade. Fish the dry fly "dead" without imparting any action or retrieve to the imitation. Cast from concealment and place the fly upstream from the feeding fish and let it drift over his lair.

Much of what a trout eats is underwater. Nymphs, wet flies, and streamers are the flies used underwater. The nymph imitates the young of an insect that hasn't completed its metamorphosis. It can be fished on a dead drift or a slow retrieve. The important thing is to keep your line tight or to watch a strike indicator that you have fastened to the butt section of your leader.

Trout take most nymphs with little energy expended. Don't expect slashing strikes. Often, a feeding trout will simply open his mouth to inhale a nymph. If the nymph happens to be your fly, you may see an almost imperceptible movement of the line. Set the hook.

Wet flies imitate the stage between nymph and emerging dry fly. These are flies that have a swept-back collar of hackle indicating the shedding of the nymphal shuck and the presence of wings. This is a type of fly that can be retrieved in a swimming manner, or let to dead drift on a tight line.

When fishing wet flies and nymphs, it is important to let the fly sink to the desired depth. When casting into current, it may be necessary to cast farther upstream to give your fly enough time for it to sink.

Streamers imitate minnows, sculpin, eels, and crayfish, all trout favorites. Fish the streamer with a drift and retrieve consistent with the behavior of the natural. Minnows travel with darting movements, staying close to cover. Sculpin stay close to the bottom. Crayfish stay even closer to the bottom and travel backwards in great thrusts of their tail.

Look for parts of the fish. A tail or a fin may catch your eye first. The trout might just look like a gray shadow against the gravel, or a hint of olive against an underwater boulder. Sometimes you can see one roll on its side, nose in the gravel. When you see a flash of silver, keep looking, you may see it again. Then go back to your car, get your rod, and tie up with a weighted nymph.

Remember that if you can see the fish, the fish can see you. Stay out of sight if you want to catch him. When stream fishing, the fish is facing upstream. You want to make your cast from downstream, behind him. Keep something between you and the fish: a bush, a tree or a boulder. Stay low. The closer you get to the fish, the lower you must be.

Walk soft, approach from downstream, and use trees and brush for concealment.

This is the essence of fly-fishing. The sight, the stalk a skillful presentation - a sip and a splash.

Reading a Trout Stream

An angler can look for fish, shadows against the rocks or watch for trout to rise, or he can fish on faith. It is about reading the water, about reaching fish in little streams and bigger rivers. You can guess the spots in the river where the fish are most likely to be found.

A trout needs three basic things: oxygen, shelter and food.

Oxygen. In general, oxygen in cold water is not a problem. What happens in the warmer months is that the trout's metabolism has increased and he needs more oxygen from the water around him. As the temperature of the water increases, the amount of oxygen that it can hold decreases. When the stream thermometer registers above 70 degrees, the trout are in danger of suffocating. Unless they can get to whitewater. The more turbulent the water, the more air is getting into it.

Shelter. Everything that will eat a fish (except another fish) comes from above. When a trout is a fingerling, a kingfisher might get him.

Lessons learned on a small stream like the Zigzag translate to bigger waters. Photo by Robert Campbell

A little older, a little bigger and blue herons will be stabbing their beaks at him. When he makes it to pan-frying size, then fishermen are interested in turning him into crispy brown fillets. So trout go where you and the birds can't see them. They will hide just off the bottom of deep holes, under cut banks, sulk in the lee of a boulder or under a fallen log where a bird cannot swoop down and take them. Unless they've been spooked, they will be within easy striking distance of dinner.

Food. The current brings much of what a trout eats to him. All that most fish below a certain size need to do is to wait. Dinner will come. But there are certain spots in a stream where the food is concentrated.

Imagine yourself sitting at a table in a busy restaurant. There is food all around you. Are you hungry? You might just go cruising from table to table picking off the choicest morsels. But that's a lot of work. Where is all the food coming from? You look around. Waiters are bringing it from the kitchen. Wouldn't it be smartest, as long as you are going to take it anyway, to intercept them as they come out? Sure, a few bites will get by you as you are eating the lobster but the small-fry need to eat too. If only so you can eat them later.

Trout aren't big thinkers, but this is how they make a living.

And this is how you should think in order to hook the biggest fish in any run. Often there is a foam or bubble line that drifts with the current. This is where the careless caddis, the unfortunate ants and grasshoppers are swept and where the larger trout line up to eat. Before you make your first cast, determine which is the best spot for a trout to wait. On a smaller stream, you can often catch the best fish first by making a good cast to the best feeding lie.

But this is the easy stuff, seeing what is happening on the surface. To really read a trout stream requires that you take all the parts that make up a particular stretch of water and see how they fit together.

Imagine this spot on the East Fork Hood River. Upstream, the water breaks over smooth stones then feeds into a deeper pool. On the far side, the water deepens where an eddy piles up leaves, bark, needles and silt. In the middle is a deep channel sloping up to shallows on the near side. Downstream, where the water slows there is a jumble of logs stacked there by floods in the last decade.

Where are the biggest fish?

Remember that a trout is both a predator and it is prey. The biggest fish will always take the best lie and that can change based on the temperature, the angle of the sun, the color of the water and the depth. During a stonefly hatch, the biggest trout might move to the head of the pool to intercept the big bugs as they drift into view. In low water when he is most vulnerable to osprey, he will back into the log jam and wait in the shadows to pick off bugs and minnows.

Imagine going below the surface and watching the bubble line from below. Where would a fish go to stay out of the heavy current yet still be close enough to take the food it wants?

Bring polarized glasses and don't string your rod until you watch the water for some time. You are reading a trout stream.

Trout fishing:
The one-knot all-day angler

What if your dad wasn't around to teach you? Or you grew up in the asphalt wasteland where the nearest fish were townie carp?

Slide a bullet sinker up the line, tie on a swivel, cut 30 inches of leader, tie it on to the other side of the swivel, tie on a No. 16 treble or a No. 10 bait hook. Open the bait jar, cut a forked stick…

That is the typical beginner's setup as advised by the typical expert but it requires a nodding acquaintance with proper weights and a certain dexterity with knots and rigging. No wonder it's so hard to catch fish if you haven't done it before.

I stopped at a 17-and-under youth fishing pond last spring to watch budding anglers in action. Aside from the fact a state trooper could have filled his ticket book with overage fishermen, it became clear what the inexperienced angler needs is better advice.

An angler with a few years behind him can set up a trout bait rig in under a minute. A novice might just go back to golf or pick up a pool cue or a fifth of Jack.

Pick a spoon that is suggestive of baitfish or other food sources. Photo by Robert Campbell

What we want are rigs that are easy to fish. Tie one knot. Go fishing.

An appropriate rod and reel combo is easy to find and can be picked up at any tackle store. The rod should be between five and seven feet long, rated for 4- to 8-pound line, and the reel should be the open-face spinning type, filled with six-pound test monofilament. Spincast Snoopy, SpongeBob and Barbie need not apply.

Now learn how to tie a knot. Use the Improved Clinch. Run the line through the eye of the lure, wind the tag six times around the line, run the tag through the loop and back through the second loop, moisten it, pull it tight. For an illustration, click on: http://www.animatedknots.com/improvedclinch/index.php

The archetype lure for the one-knot angler must be the 1/6-ounce Rooster Tail spinner. Buy it in brown or black and take it to the lake. Cast and retrieve with a little twitch to get the blade revolving about the shaft. If it's not spinning it won't catch a thing. Crank just fast enough to get the blade spinning and keep it off the bottom. No faster. Move from spot to spot till you find the fish.

You're going to lose gear. If you're not snagging up, you're not fishing where the fish are. If you can't pop the lure free, point the rod at the lure and back up with one hand on the spool to break the line. Reel it in, trim off the frayed end and tie that Improved Clinch again.

Another good spinner is the Mack's Lure Promise Keeper. The one you want for hatchery rainbows is the 1/8-ounce model in a frog pattern or in black with a red dot.

These lures target the aggressive fish in any pod of trout, the ones most likely to feed on baitfish and minnows.

An even easier lure to fish is a crankbait like Worden's Timber Tiger. Try the Delta Craw or Rainbow Trout pattern in the DC-2 or DC-3 configuration. These plastic-lipped baits dive when they're cranked. They are a good bet too, when trolled 60 feet behind the boat. In deeper water, use the DC-8 or greater rating.

When fishing a river for trout, consider another one-knot option. Tie a small jig head on to the main line then slip a bubblegum pink or an orange skirted tube like Outlaw Bait's 2.25-inch Steelie Tube over the head of the jig. Cast it upstream then hold the rod high and let the jig bounce along the bottom.

The trick is to use these lures with either 4-pound or 6-pound test main line. Any heavier and fish will spook.

One-knot fishing targets the bigger fish, the predators that feed on minnows. And a day's worth of tackle can fit in one pocket-size box. If you haven't exhausted your angling budget yet, buy a landing net. You're going to need it.

Fly & Bubble Fishing

To fish a fly on spinning tackle, use a casting bubble. It must be the type that can be filled with water, which provides the weight necessary for long-distance casting. Whether fishing on the surface or below the surface, the best choice is the medium-size, clear plastic bubble.

Slide the bubble over your main line and tie on a No. 12 black barrel swivel. Knot a three- to four-foot, four-pound test leader to your barrel swivel, then tie on the fly. For starters, use a wet fly such as a No. 10 Prince Nymph or black Woolly Bugger or red tag Woolly Worm.

The reel should be filled with six-pound test monofilament. On the cast, stop the bubble right before it hits the water. The momentum will swing the fly or flies into line. Tighten up the line then let the flies settle into the water column. Now start to reel. Retrieve in stops and starts. Watch the surface for a swirl behind the float. If you see a strike, set the hook even if you don't feel the bite.

Once the art of the cast and retrieve are mastered, try a second fly on the line. Tie eighteen inches of leader (fluorocarbon is the most stealthy) to the bend of the hook then knot on another fly. Experiment with a streamer fly or a dragonfly nymph behind a smaller bug. Sometimes the fishing is faster when the trout have choices. Sometimes an angler can catch two fish on the same cast.

James Flaherty with a Boulder Lake brook trout. Photo by Gary Lewis

Catch & Release

Anyone who decides to turn a fish loose has an obligation to return it to the water, giving it as good a chance to survive as possible. From the moment you hook a fish to the instant when it kicks away from your cradled hands, your highest duty is to preserve its life. If not, then preaching the mantra of catch and release is idle talk.

A small percentage of released fish die, no matter how much care is taken during the fight and subsequent handling. Often, it is their own will to throw the hook that kills them. Sometimes, it is the way they are hooked that seals their fate.

Being sensitive to the fragility of life, the careful angler can reduce to a tiny fraction the number of fish that die after being hooked and released. It starts with the method of take. Fish that are caught on bait are most vulnerable. Often the hook is taken deeper in the mouth, or almost in the stomach if the fish is allowed to swallow the bait before the hook is set.

When treble hooks are used, the potential for damage is increased, as more hooks can create more wounds. If the fish is bleeding, the chances that it will die are increased. Pinching the barbs down ensures that a smaller wound will be created.

At the end of the battle, the fish should not be removed from the water if the intent is to let it go. Avoid using a net, if you can. If you must use a net, use one made of rubber which won't remove the fish's essential protective slime. Don't touch the eyes or the gills. Reach down and slip the hook out. If the fish has taken the hook deep, cut the line and trust the fish's stomach acids to destroy the hook in a few days. The fish still has a good chance of survival if you handle it with care.

If a picture is desired, have the cameraman ready to snap the instant it is lifted from the water.

Next, point the fish upstream and cradle it in both hands, underwater. Gently rock it back and forth to prompt the opening and closing of the gills in the normal breathing pattern. Be patient, wait until the fish begins to move on its own again. If the fish begins to lean one way or the other, keep rocking it until, rested, it kicks away.

Give it as much time as it takes to swim away under its own power. The future of your fishing might depend on your patience.

As much as possible, keep wild fish in the water and revive them at their own pace.

Fly Shops & Tackle Stores of Mount Hood Country

The Gorge Fly Shop, Hood River

Fin and Fire, Redmond

Confluence Fly Shop, Bend

Fly and Field, Bend

Fly Shops & Tackle Stores of Mount Hood Country

Patient Angler, Bend

Gorge Outfitters, Rufus

Flyfishing Strategies, The Dalles

Fisherman's Marine and Outdoors, Oregon City

Oregon Fishing Club

Scenes from Mount Hood Country

Index of Advertisers

About the Authors

Gary Lewis learned to fish on the Kalama River and landed his first steelhead on the North Fork Lewis River. He moved to Oregon at the age of 19 and began to fish the Clackamas, the Sandy and Eagle Creek on a regular basis. Today he lives a stone's throw from the Deschutes in Central Oregon.

Lewis is an outdoor writer, speaker, photographer and TV host who has hunted and fished in seven countries and across the United States. He is twice past president of the Northwest Outdoor Writers Association (NOWA) and is a recipient of NOWA's prestigious Enos Bradner Award.

Lewis is host of Frontier Unlimited, a TV show, and is also the author of 15 books.

Lewis is a columnist for The Bend Bulletin, a Contributing Editor for Successful Hunter magazine and a humor columnist for Bear Hunting magazine and a regular contributor for many other magazines and newspapers. His stories have appeared in Sports Afield, Rifle, Successful Hunter, African Hunting Gazette, Boating Sportsman, Traditional Bowhunter, Mule Deer, African Hunter, Cascades East, Flyfishing and Tying Journal, Washington-Oregon Game & Fish, Oregon Hunter, SalmonTroutSteelheader and more.

Lewis is happily married to his wife of 27 years, Merrilee, and together they have three daughters, all accomplished with spinning gear and fly rod.

Robert H. Campbell is a lifelong Oregonian and an award-winning outdoor writer. While his work has appeared in many different regional magazines, he is a regular contributor to Salmon Trout Steelheader. His first book, Illustrated Rigging, has remained on the best seller list of Frank Amato Publications since its release in 2007.

Since his father introduced him to the quiet sport of angling at an early age, Robert has been enamored of wild rivers, primeval forests and the creatures that dwell in each. He is especially fond of steelhead: "Steelhead are an icon of the land and water that are dear to me. They are representative of the place where I live, my family history and healthy rivers. I love them most for their wildness, and, for the amazing places that they take me."

Robert grew up on the west side of Portland, Oregon, and has spent a good part of his life working, playing and living in the Mount Hood Country. He currently lives in western Oregon in close proximity to several salmon and steelhead rivers, including the stream where he caught his very first winter steelhead at the age of five. Some of his favorite places to fish are the Deschutes and Sandy Rivers, Timothy Lake, any coastal stream big or small, and Elk Lake near Bend, Oregon.

Robert is happily married to his wife of 17 years, Katherine, and has two smart, funny, tough, beautiful daughters who also share his love of Oregon's wild places.

CPSIA information can be obtained at www.ICGtesting.com
Printed in the USA
LVOW01s0803030715

444780LV00001B/1/P